Nonachieving Students At Risk:

School, Family, and Community Intervention

by Harry W. Sartain

nea PROFE*JONAL*LIBRARY
National Education Association
Washington, D.C.

Printing History
    First Printing: September 1989

Note

The opinions expressed in this publication should not be construed as representing the policy or position of the National Education Association. Materials published by the NEA Professional Library are intended to be discussion documents for educators who are concerned with specialized interests of the profession.

Library of Congress Cataloging-in-Publication Data

Sartain, Harry Wendell.
    Nonachieving students at risk : school, family, and community
intervention / Harry W. Sartain.
        p.   cm. — (Analysis and action series)
    Bibliography: p.
    ISBN 0–8106–3074–5
    1. Underachievers—United States.   2. Slow learning children—
United States.   3. Motivation in education.   I. Title.
II. Series.
LC4691.S27   1989
371.92'6—dc20   89–36128
                                                                      CIP

CONTENTS

The Author

Harry W. Sartain is Professor, School of Education, University of Pittsburgh, Pennsylvania. He has both taught and supervised on the elementary and middle school level. Dr. Sartain is the author of approximately 90 publications.

The Advisory Panel

Carl Downing, Professor of Elementary Education, Central State University, Edmond, Oklahoma

Margaret Hardesty-Day, Teacher, Russellville Middle School, Kentucky

Curtis J. Gilbertson, Byron Elementary School, Minnesota

Chapter 1

STUDENTS AT RISK: CRISIS IN CLASSROOM AND COMMUNITY

More than one-fourth of the children in American schools are caught in binds that put them at risk of great frustration, depression, extreme anger, antisocial attitudes, drug and alcohol dependence, delinquency, possible suicide, school failure, dropping out of school, and future unemployment. They are in such desperate situations because of limited aspirations or aptitudes, inadequate parenting, and inflexible academic school programs that are not suited to their needs.

In early America, students who were not successful in school quickly quit and found gainful work on farms. Today, less than 4 percent of the population is engaged in America's bounteous agricultural production. During the past century, millions moved to the cities to work in booming mills and factories. But now millions of factory jobs have been lost because Americans can import products more cheaply from foreign countries that have low labor costs. Jobs available in America today require more education and skill than formerly (134),* and hundreds of thousands of unemployed people do not have the competencies required for employment.

Many students today become discouraged about education very early because of unfair competition in graded schools where all are expected to learn at the same rate with equal success. They often quit trying at the elementary level, and then join an alienated group where they become social problems before dropping out as soon as the law will allow. Others become discouraged because of lack of parental support, or because schools do not offer them what they feel they need—vocational training for jobs that will lead to a satisfying life. Still others are impatient and uncooperative because schooling now takes so long that it interferes with normal human growth and the needs for mature responsibility, sex, and independence. Some students do not see enough benefit in education to compensate for delayed gratification of desires.

As the only organized social institution, other than the home, that

---

*Numbers in parentheses appearing in the text refer to the Bibliography beginning on page 48.

can touch all young people, the school must offer leadership in taking drastic steps to redirect the values of 25 to 35 percent of today's youth. Schools must help teachers become more sensitive to students' feelings and problems, must make individual uniqueness appreciated instead of penalized, must make flexible school progress a normal expectation, and must involve parents in giving support to learning. Educators need to recognize that just as every student does not have the aptitude to become an opera singer or a professional football player, everybody does not have high scholarly interest and aptitudes as did the small percentage who remained in school 75 years ago. Educators must institute more alternative and vocational programs to provide for the 25 percent of students who will not go on to college (257).

If such steps are not taken, the increasing number of students at risk eventually can put the whole American society at risk.

DEFINITION

Who are the students at risk? In the educator's view, students at risk are children of school age, who, because of one or more factors in a syndrome of disadvantageous traits, behaviors, and circumstances, are in danger of being unsuccessful in school and/or in danger of becoming enmeshed in personally debilitating social, emotional, physical, or economic difficulties currently or in the near future.

These problems may have their roots in infancy and usually develop in home, school, and community situations that occur long before the unfortunate behaviors become highly visible in later school years. Among the groups of disadvantageous factors that may, if occurring to an abnormal degree, be related to the individual's at-risk status are the following:

- *Limited Background Attainments*—Inadequate language development, lack of family experience to develop normal concepts and positive attitudes, inadequate early school learning, lack of normal literacy, lack of other necessary skills.
- *Personal Development Difficulties*—Vision or hearing deficiencies, other physical handicaps, subtle learning disabilities, irresponsible sexual activity.
- *Physical Deprivation*—Hunger, malnutrition, poor housing, homelessness, inadequate clothing.
- *Disease and Illness*—Dental problems, frequent infections, AIDS, other chronic diseases, epilepsy.
- *Neglect or Abuse*—Loss of one or both parents, lack of social-emotional support from family, maltreatment, inappropriate placement

for instruction, negative labeling by school or others, being threatened or ridiculed for lack of achievement or other difficulties.

- *Emotional Handicaps*—Fearfulness, depression, social withdrawal, suicidal tendencies, excessive irritability or anger, lack of emotional bonding (sociopathology), unusually aggressive feelings.
- *Nonscholarly Tendencies*—Unsuitable aptitude for assigned tasks, nonscholarly interests, dislike for school experiences or school personnel.
- *Substance Addiction*—Frequent use of drugs, alcohol, or tobacco.
- *Antisocial Tendencies*—Hostility, uncooperative behavior, frequent absence, deceptiveness, strongly biased/discriminatory behavior related to race or other human qualities, membership in an alienated subculture, physical/verbal abusiveness, delinquency, criminality.

While some of these young people are highly visible, others may function quietly, unhappily, and inadequately without all of their problems being noticed unless teachers are alert.

7

Chapter 2

ROOTS OF THE PROBLEM

It is not possible to establish clear-cut, unrelated causes for different types of risk problems because causal factors often are related and overlapping. For this discussion, the roots of the problem will be classified quite roughly under: (a) Personal Psychological Factors, (b) Family Environment Factors, (c) Community Environment Factors, and (d) School Environment Factors.

Omitted from the above classification is the significant area of genetic factors. These are being omitted because of the scope of a book of this size. Even so, the complex aspects of nature versus nurture, intelligence testing, biogenetics, and delinquency are critical to an understanding of the roots of the problem and it is hoped that an independent study of the literature will be pursued by the readers of this work. These references in the Bibliography will be especially pertinent: 82, 86, 125, 146, 170, 222, 240, 246. Special attention must be drawn to a major, recent study by Paul Bouchard (119) focused on a study of more than 300 pairs of twins. The conclusions by Bouchard's research team that inherited aptitudes and tendencies should be credited with about 50 percent of behavior (70% of academic growth) are very useful in considering sources of problems of students at risk.

PERSONAL/PSYCHOLOGICAL FACTORS

Some of the factors that seem to cause students to function in ways that put them at risk are personal characteristics that cannot be said to have either only genetic or only environmental roots. Among these are learning style, learning disability, impaired ego function, emotional disturbance, low aspiration/motivation, and the antisocial personality disorder. All can seriously affect a student's learning.

Learning Styles

Keefe says that, "Learning styles are cognitive, affective, and physiological traits that serve as relatively stable indicators of how learners perceive, interact with, and respond to the learning environment" (139, p.

44). Of the several assessment tools, the *Learning Style Inventory* by Dunn, Dunn, and Price is most used. Price (187) has described the research done in determining what should be included in the inventory, and Griggs (97) has summarized the coverage in somewhat this manner: (1) Environmental stimuli: light, sound, temperature, design; (2) Emotional stimuli: structure, persistence, motivation, responsibility; (3) Sociological stimuli: pairs, peers, adults, self, group, varied; (4) Physical stimuli: perceptual strengths (auditory, visual, tactual, kinesthetic), mobility, intake, time of day; and (5) Psychological stimuli: global/analytic, impulsive/reflective, cerebral dominance.

Use of a cognitive styles inventory usually requires students to state preferences for the various factors in the learning situation. Pies (185), found however, in working with 177 low-socioeconomic status Black children in grades 3 through 6, that children did not clearly perceive their own learning styles, while their teachers could perceive the styles and predict student achievement.

Early studies on adapting instruction to learning style in reading were not encouraging (89), but the surge of research from the late '70s through the '80s has been more promising. Dunn has summarized research showing that learning style can predict reading achievement better than IQ. She says the evidence shows, "that youngster's attitudes about their schools, their teachers, and learning improve when they are taught by methods, resources, or programs that respond to their unique characteristics" (61, p. 144). Anthony (8) used Renzulli and Smith's learning styles inventory, an attitude scale, and the California Achievement Tests to examine progress of 193 fifth-grade pupils when their learning styles were or were not in congruence with teaching styles of eight teachers. She considered congruence on such instructional procedures as project work, simulations, drill with recitations, peer teaching, discussion, teaching games, and independent study. She found that students achieved higher when their learning styles were congruent with teaching styles on five factors. Congruence in two areas resulted in higher attitude scores.

Somewhat contrary to statements of stability in learning styles, Keefe (140) says that perceptual preference seems to evolve for most students from tactual-kinesthetic to visual and aural as the learner matures. Carbo concluded that "Young students tend to be global rather than analytic. They learn best when information is presented as a gestalt or whole. Many may not be ready for the step-by-step presentation of phonic rules until second or third grades" (36, p. 131).

In Carbo's study of learning styles of 293 students in grades 2, 4, 6, and 8, she identified 10 elements of reading style and related them to age levels. Second-graders had relatively higher preferences for tactual

9

and kinesthetic stimuli than students at higher levels. They also expressed need for more intake and mobility. Second-graders were highly teacher-motivated and preferred to read in groups more than alone. At a higher level, strength in the visual modality was shown, and students were able, as shown in other studies, to learn well through the auditory sense at grades 5 and 6 (36).

Carbo also found that a particularly effective method of teaching reading to young children was the "whole-word, global approach . . . tape-recorded storybooks followed by games about the books. With this method, children see and hear words simultaneously within the context of high-interest stories and then practice the vocabulary presented in game form" (36, p. 131). This process significantly increased comprehension and vocabulary of both beginning readers and disabled readers.

The importance of observing differences in learning styles of different ethnic groups was demonstrated by Andera and Atwell (5). They found that American Indian children had problems in beginning to use school communication because their native style is less dominated by a leader and their communication is directed to listeners differently. Also, they consider it insulting to stare at another person.

Learning Disabilities

Learning disabilities might be considered in direct relationship with learning styles, because learning disabled (LD) students do learn if taught with appropriate techniques. Educators noticed symbol-processing problems originally when a good rural student suddenly became a problem learner after being kicked in the head by a horse. Medical persons long had noted that an adult often has memory and learning difficulties after a stroke. Then psychologists observed pupils who had not had such injuries, but had similar types of learning difficulties. Several definitions of learning disabilities have been offered, and one agreed on in 1981 by a half-dozen professional groups follows:

> Learning disabilities is a generic term that refers to a heterogeneous group of disorders manifested by significant difficulties in the acquisition and use of listening, speaking, reading, writing, reasoning or mathematical abilities. These disorders are intrinsic to the individual and presumed to be due to central nervous system dysfunction. Even though a learning disability may occur concomitantly with other handicapping conditions (e.g., sensory impairment, mental retardation, social and emotional disturbance) or environmental influences (e.g., cultural differences, insufficient-inappropriate instruction, psychogenic factors), it is not the direct result of those conditions or influences. (141, p. 7)

Researchers say some possible causes for learning disability are genetic, neurological injury, biochemical problems, and social-emotional stress. Because learning disability causes anything from mild to acute difficulties in learning, it obviously can be a serious factor in putting students at risk of failure. For example, approximately 20 percent of the severe reading disabilities are caused by learning disability (202).

Because of widely varying diagnostic standards, the stated numbers of learning disability cases fluctuate wildly, rising considerably whenever special funds are available for treatment. Probably the estimate by the Office of Special Education that 1 to 3 percent of school children suffer from learning disabilities is the most accurate. In 1984, however, more than 4 percent of public school children were in special learning disability classes. Because LD so often has not been diagnosed and treated properly in the school curriculum, correctional authorities often estimate that as many as half of penitentiary inmates have learning disabilities. The National Institute of Juvenile Justice and Delinquency Prevention has reported that 36.5, or one-third, of boys adjudicated as delinquent are learning disabled (186). Interestingly, as many as four to six times as many boys are diagnosed learning disabled as girls (157).

Impaired Ego Function and Low Motivation

Teachers wonder why some children don't try harder, but students, even those having adequate aptitudes, may put inadequate effort into their schoolwork because of the related factors of inadequate self-concepts, low aspirations, low motivation, inadequate conative (drive) development, and negative values.

Studies repeatedly have shown that students who underachieve in comparison with others in their classes, have lower self-concepts and lower feelings of self-worth, (162, 189). In a seven-year study, Coopersmith (52) found three conditions that related to development of positive self-esteem. Briefly, they are (1) nearly total acceptance of the child by its parents—expression of much warmth and love and acceptance of child behavior, making the child feel of personal importance; (2) clearly defined and enforced limits—reasonable rules and demands firmly enforced and rewarded, with any necessary punishment perceived as justified; and (3) respect and latitude for individual action—sharing of views and opinions along with noncoercive treatment of behavior that is within the limits of clearly established rules (52).

Research reveals that teachers also affect children's self-perceptions. "Students who feel they are liked and respected by their teachers have higher self-concepts, while those who believe they are disliked by their

11

teachers are more dissatisfied with themselves" (214, p. 18). Several researchers have observed that the attainment of positive student self-concepts is related to supportive teacher behaviors such as calm, accepting interaction, use of humor, and a low degree of negative evaluation and grim domination (214). Harsh, unsympathetic criticism by either teachers or parents regularly is found to be related to impairment of ego function, lowering the child's self-esteem.

Weiner (248) and his associates found that highly motivated students and those having low motivation tend to attribute their levels of success to different causes. Highly motivated students attribute success to having high ability, over which they have no control, and their failures to lack of effort, which they can control and improve. Poorly motivated students tend to attribute their successes to uncontrollable factors such as luck, while their lack of success is attributed to low capability, also uncontrollable (248). Even students who have good aptitude but infrequent success may develop this low regard for themselves. "Ability attributions have the greatest impact on self-esteem, and so individuals tend to feel best when they attribute success to ability, and worst when failure is attributed to lack of ability" (255, p. 425). Low self-esteem in learning is debilitating because "motivation to pursue a goal is determined by the expectancy one has of attaining that goal and the value one places on attaining it" (255, p. 424). And it is easy to rationalize that an educational goal is not of great value if one feels one cannot attain it.

Students' unwillingness to attempt challenging tasks is explained also by Covington's concept of the self-worth motive (53). This is based on the human need to maintain self-respect, a positive self-image. Decisions about attempts and actions usually are made with a view to protecting one's self-image; nobody wants to be caught short in front of others or even in his or her own view. Therefore, if a student has any doubt about his or her ability to succeed at a task such as an academic assignment, it is safer to protect the ego by refusing to do the assignment than to risk inadequate performance in attempting it.

School experiences seem to have different effects on various students' self-images and consequent willingness to work. The more successful students tend to develop stronger self-concepts as the years of schooling pass, while the less successful lose in self-concept (214). Life is a vicious circle for lower achievers because, unless something intervenes to change the course, their loss in self-confidence can make them feel helpless, or can make them feel forced into a life of crime. Impaired ego-function is very common in juvenile delinquents (146).

Students adapt their aspirations not only to their self-images, but also to perceived opportunities in relation to their socioeconomic heritage.

Cooks (50) studied the aspirations and plans of a very large number of Black students in senior high schools. She found that they were approaching their futures cautiously, looking carefully at the opportunities available in American society. Their plans were heavily influenced by the curriculum tracks they followed, their school grades, their perceived academic abilities, and the social and financial values they placed on further education. The single most important factor was the curriculum track, perhaps either because it represented their interests or they may have felt it signified something about their capabilities.

Atman (10) found that goal-oriented behaviors of students in grades 6, 7, and 8 distinguish those who are achieving from those who are not. The nonachievers appear to lack conative development, desire, and practice in striving. In the 1700s, conation was considered to be one of the important domains for development, along with the cognitive and the affective, but it has not appeared in educational objectives for some time. Recently, much research has focused on goal development in students, and Atman has identified steps by which successful students manifest goal-oriented efforts. They include recognizing a problem, setting a goal, visualizing how to achieve the goal, organizing, beginning to make it happen, pushing forward without procrastination, concluding the activity, and fitting the achievement into a long-range sense of purpose (10).

Emotional Problems

A low self-concept can be one of the symptoms of a still more serious problem—depression. In summarizing research, Hughes (122) says that the onset of a depressive episode is indicated by evidence every day for two weeks of at least five of the following: (1) feelings of worthlessness or inappropriate guilt, (2) depressed or irritable mood, (3) significant change in appetite or weight, (4) markedly diminished interest or pleasure in most activities, (5) daily insomnia or hypersomnia, (6) psychomotor agitation or retardation, (7) unusual fatigue, (8) indecisiveness or inability to concentrate, and (9) recurrent thoughts of death or suicide (122).

Reynolds (193) and his colleagues conducted epidemiologic studies of over 8,000 young people in public and private schools, and concluded that 14 percent of children in grades 4 to 6 and 16 percent of those in grades above 6 were clinically depressed. At the higher levels, another 18 percent had borderline problems. It is estimated that between three and six million children and adolescents in the United States suffer from recognized or unrecognized depression (181).

In addition to problems of concentration on schoolwork, depressed children are likely to be socially withdrawn (122). Among young people first admitted to a psychiatric facility, depression is the most common symptom for those manifesting suicidal thoughts or acts, while anger is the most common symptom of others (122)

Rosenthal and Rosenthal (198) observed that suicidal preschool children, in addition to depressive symptoms, tend to direct aggression against themselves, to run away, and to express little sensitivity to pain after injury. They are likely to be unwanted children, to feel abandonment and despair. Despite sometimes being victims of child abuse, they have fantasies of family reunion and a better life.

Genetic studies in recent years show that a particular hereditary chromosome variation can provide a predisposition toward some types of depression. And "a history of suicide in a family is a significant risk factor for suicide . . . Parents of suicidal children often are depressed and suicidal" (181, p. 27). Researchers noted that, "Children and adolescents with a biological predisposition to depression may be at high risk for suicide when dealing with psychological and social stress" (181, p. 28).

Depressed individuals are characterized not only by negative views of themselves, but by a negative view of the world and the future (122). While they need much experience with success in order to develop positive feelings, their cognitive functions do not operate in a manner that permits them readily to gain self-esteem from successes in the normal way. Because of their negative thinking, they tend to attribute their successes to uncontrollable external factors instead of to their own merit. Consequently, experience with success does not necessarily make them more confident when they face a similar task in the future (122).

Hyperactivity and Disruptive Behavior

Sometimes a child does not participate freely in a group because of any of a variety of social anxieties. Children, as implied previously, are afraid of losing face. Collier (46) described how one psychologist surveyed children in relation to their fears, and found that a child is more fearful about receiving a bad report card or having a toilet accident than about having surgery. They fear being sent to the principal's office more than going to the dentist. It distresses them to be seen as stupid, unattractive, or dishonest. Their greatest anxiety is about losing a parent.

More noticeable to the busy teacher is the hyperactive child. This youngster runs around the room, annoys other students, talks, fidgets, becomes involved in irrelevant activities, and frequently fails to complete schoolwork at the appropriate level for his or her aptitude. "Hyperactivi-

14

ty is one of the most commonly identified behavioral problems of children, with estimates of the incidence ranging from about 3 percent to as high as 20 percent. Boys are three to ten times more likely to be labeled hyperactive than girls" (254, p. 103).

Young children, of course, are naturally restless, but the hyperactive child is far more mobile than the average. Excessive activity may diminish in middle or higher grades, while difficulty in maintaining attention to tasks may continue. Adults who have had a history of hyperactivity and serious attention difficulties "tend to exhibit personality problems and may be predisposed to alcoholism" (122, p. 130).

There is little agreement on the cause of hyperactive, impulsive behavior. Various researchers see its origins as genetic, as neurological damage, or as induced by environmental stress. Others feel that such behavior tendencies result from deficiencies in the cognitive mechanisms that regulate attention and inhibit inappropriate movement (122).

There is agreement, however, that impulsive hyperactivity is one of the predictors of juvenile delinquency. Another predictor of future delinquency and a great concern in the classroom is behavior that is particularly aggressive—of the student who is rebellious, is argumentative, makes derogatory remarks, threatens others, and starts fights. Between one-third and one-half of the students referred for psychological services are hyperactive (122).

While depressed individuals are burdened with feelings of guilt, "unsocialized conduct-oriented children are unconcerned with the effects of their behavior on others and feel little remorse or guilt over their actions" (122, p. 160). Although some aggression is normal in toddlers, it usually lessens with socialization. If it is not reduced by normal growth, it tends to remain a stable characteristic of the individual (122). Antisocial, aggressive students usually are unpopular with their peers. Sometimes, obviously, they have earned this unpopularity. At other times, it appears that they may have become antisocial because they were rejected (20).

Antisocial behavior usually is associated with inadequate school achievement. One team of researchers (200) found that one-fourth of slow readers demonstrated antisocial behavior, while a third of all conduct-disordered children had reading disabilities.

Antisocial Personality Disorder

The students at risk who are most dangerous to society are those having an antisocial personality disorder (APD), often referred to as psychopaths or sociopaths, who lack conscience. Some of the traits that these character-disturbed children exhibit include lack of ability to give and receive affection, self-destructive behavior, cruelty to others and to pets, stealing, hoarding, extreme control problems, lack of long-term friends, preoccupation with fire and blood, superficial attractiveness and friendliness to strangers, and crazy lying (44, 161). As they mature into full-fledged psychopaths, they add traits of glibness and superficial charm, grandiose sense of self-worth, need for stimulation to avoid boredom, manipulative behaviors, shallow feelings, parasitic lifestyle, promiscuous sex activity, irresponsibility, impulsivity, lack of realistic planning, and criminal versatility (104, 161). "Trust, love, loyalty, and teamwork are incompatible with their way of life. They scorn and exploit most people who are kind, trusting, hardworking, and honest" (161, p. 9).

Estimated at perhaps 5 percent of the population, character-disturbed children are the largest category among severely disturbed youth, and more boys become psychopathic than girls (161). A study of 9,949 Philadelphia males revealed that 34.9 percent had been involved with the police by age 18 (260). Of this group, 6.3 percent were chronic offenders, and this small number of chronic cases was responsible for at least 51.9 percent of all crimes reported (161). Apparently the individuals most likely to have real antisocial personality disorders are extreme problems to society.

Research by Cline (44), by Magid and McKelvey (161), and by others indicates that the major cause of antisocial personality disorder is inadequate emotional attachment, or failure of the infant to bond emotionally with a parent or other significant adult.

Antisocial personality disorder occurs when the infant does not learn to trust another person within about the first four months of life (161). The first stage in the process is for the infant to feel a need, such as a need for milk. Being annoyed by its discomfort, the infant moves into Stage 2 with a rage reaction, such as crying or flailing its limbs. After time is taken for its rage signals to be noticed by the parent, Stage 3, the gratification of the need by a recognized adult and relief of distress occurs in the normal situation. This is accompanied by eye contact, patting, encouraging words, smiles, and other behaviors that make the infant feel loved. Normally Stage 4 follows, in which the infant feels trust in the adult and increases his or her emotional bonding with that person (161).

In the unhealthy situation, however, the child is neglected, is verbally or physically abused, is not given any gratification until after an abnormal delay, or is given needed attention by somebody perceived as a stranger. Instead of acquiring trust in the parent, the infant then experiences and internalizes overwhelming rage and distrust of other humans

16

(161). Competent treatment must be provided by age 7 in order to have a good chance of success (245).

The severity of the antisocial personality disorder differs with individuals and circumstances, but Hirschi (118) found, in studying 5,000 boys, that the more a child is attached to and identifies with his parents, the less likelihood there is for delinquency. In summarizing research, Hurley (123) also found that youths without close family bonds are more likely to experiment with delinquency. He noted that when those lacking close family bonding are placed in homes for delinquents, they usually bond with other antisocial youths like themselves, thereby reinforcing delinquent behavior. "Charles Manson was neglected and used as a child, setting the stage for the conscienceless adult he was to become" (161, p. 23).

FAMILY ENVIRONMENT FACTORS

Among family factors affecting children's education and success are child care, family attitudes and values, parental role-modeling and guidance, family tensions, and family economics. Downing and Leong (58) have quoted an English researcher in support of this contention:

> Factors in the home environment are overwhelmingly more important than those of the neighborhood or the school. Of these home influences, factors of maternal care and of parental attitude to education, to school, and to books, are of greater significance than social class and occupational level. (259, p. 227)

Many children live in single-parent families, and 50 percent of the rest have both parents working" (247, p. 112). Few families are extended to include grandparents in the home, and older students often lack any family member to go to for advice. On the average, in 1970, family members spent about 15 minutes a day interacting, and some of that was confrontational. "Some middle-class fathers spend no more than a few minutes a week interacting with each child" (247, p. 112).

Child Care and Child Abuse

The importance of providing adequate food, shelter, and clothing in order to give children an opportunity to learn and succeed in school is obvious. Malnutrition or sensory deprivation during the early months and years can have lasting consequences for inadequate mental development (121). Good home experiences of love, perceptual stimulation, conversation, and responsibiltiy provide support for language development, self-confidence, and security (107).

17

Unfortunately, between 1900 and 1973 the number of reports of child abuse quadrupled (238). This may have been because of more accurate reporting, or because of a change in lifestyles, involving pornographic films and the use of young girls seductively in TV films and advertising. Between 60 and 75 percent of the child abuse cases now reported are of the sex abuse type, and in the single year from 1983 to 1984, the number of sex abuse cases reported increased 50 percent from 35,014 to 55,596. In the same period, child abuse reports rose 16 percent, from 828,417 to 958,590 (238). Boys as well as girls are sexually abused, with an estimated 2.5 to 5.0 percent of boys under age 13 having had sexual experiences with adults (72).

Finkelhor (72) found a higher incidence of sexual abuse in families having stepfathers, perhaps because of the number of men with whom the mother associated before remarriage. In interviewing abusive and nonabusive mothers, Golub (88) found that the two types were about equally angry and disliked the disapproved behavior equally. Abusive mothers, however, were more inclined to feel the disliked behavior was intentional and more serious. Also, they expressed less positive attitudes toward their children.

Some children can survive abuse while retaining their social problem-solving skills (152); others seem to suffer serious effects. Those suffering emotional abuse, such as belittling and comments expressing rejection, often exhibit behaviors of withdrawal, extremes in emotion, destructive behavior, inordinate attention to details, cheating, cruelty, thumbsucking, rocking, anorexia nervosa, and delinquency (238). Additional behaviors common among those who are bruised, burned, or otherwise physically abused, are fearfulness, overcompliance, being at school too early or late, accident proneness, under achievement, regressiveness, inability to form good peer relationships, extreme hostility and aggressiveness, and appearance of incorrigibility (238). A few of the sex abuse indicators are frequent urinary infections, inordinate gifts received, great secrecy, unusual sex knowledge, unusual worldliness, inferior feelings, crying, and even suicide attempts (238).

Child neglect or abuse can cause impaired ego function, and antisocial personality disorders. These, in turn, result in poor academic achievement and further problems.

Family Attitudes and Values

Young children tend to achieve at higher levels when they are aware of their parents' interest, and they tend to inculcate the values their parents display. When parents show that their attitudes toward schools are negative, that they have little interest in their children's schoolwork or that they do not place special value on good work habits, the effect on school achievement almost always is negative (58).

One researcher (56), tabulated the frequency of parents' visits to the school as part of the evidence of their interest, and concluded that children whose parents were most interested had the highest reading achievement. He also found that 70 percent of children of interested parents were rated as hard workers, while only 33 percent of disinterested parents' children were so rated. In a related study, a team (57) found that between ages 11 and 15 the reading levels of children having interested parents continued to improve, while achievement of children of disinterested parents tended to deteriorate.

Parents who read frequently and have many good books and magazines in the home demonstrate values that tend to be assimilated by their children (201). The home reading environment seems to have more effect on a child's reading attitudes than socioeconomic status (255). A writer concerned about value development through character education in the home expresses concern that "traditional agents of character education have been weakened by the fluidity and heterogeneity of American society" (156). Another summarizes events briefly: "In less than 50 years, America has virtually abandoned the work ethic that was a cornerstone of this society and accepted a hedonistic philosophy... Many of us have dropped out from everything—marriage, parenting, voting, churchgoing, paying taxes, saving for the future... Why should we be surprised that our young people drop out?" (150, p. 62).

Parental Guidance and Role-Modeling

Guidance and directions given by parents, if they do not antagonize the student, tend to lead the youngster toward higher achievement. In studying Mexican-American children, Henderson (112) found that the amount of parent pressure for achievement correlated slightly higher with achievement scores than IQ. Perhaps because of lack of adequate parent guidance, high school students who are from low-income homes and are not high achievers spend more time on physical activities, including odd jobs, than do good readers (92). The monitoring of television viewing is one area in which parental guidance can be important; studies show excessive watching is always detrimental to reading achievement. The number of hours per day found to be definitely detrimental was three in one review (17) and four in two others (175, 208). The negative effect differs, however, in relation to age and ability. Up to age 9, children can watch three or four hours without academic loss (208), per-

19

haps because whatever else they would do with the time would not benefit achievement significantly, and the TV might provide some useful background information. By age 13, however, it appears that there is some reduction in achievement if a student views TV more than one or two hours daily (208).

Students having the highest academic aptitudes are the ones to suffer the most academically from excessive TV watching. In one study (172), there was no apparent reduced achievement for heavy watchers in the low- and average-intelligence range. This, again, could be because these students would not ordinarily use the time for something more educational. Many students watch 6 to 7 hours a day, with students of low-socioeconomic status watching the most (208).

Quality of programs needs to be monitored as much as quantity. Some research shows a negative relation between reading achievement and viewing TV programs such as cartoons, situation comedies, and adventure (17). One study of TV viewing by 900 third-graders revealed a positive correlation between the violence of preferred programs and the aggressive behavior of certain children. A four-year study of tenth-grade boys showed that those identified as most aggressive preferred violent behavior on television more than nonviolent students (231).

While these correlations with aggression do not prove causality, vicarious experiences sometimes do serve as an excuse for some to act out (253).

Thousands of children speak a language other than English that they have learned at home before coming to school. The use of bilingual programs in classes is a burning issue, but research on the topic so far is not very helpful. So far, "research generally shows higher dropout rates among students enrolled in bilingual programs, though it remains difficult to disentangle cause and effect" (100, p. 260).

Disorganized and Disrupted Homes

Research usually finds a positive relationship between stable homes and good achievement, and between unstable homes and delinquency (108). While many children do well in spite of disruption, teachers need to weigh such matters in counseling.

The U.S. divorce rate is about 2,300,000 per year, leaving approximately 24 percent of all children under 18 living in single-parent families (171), but 40 percent of Black children live in single-parent homes (156). (Others disagree, saying 11 percent (264) or 40 percent (247) of all live in single-parent homes.) Children are being raised by 700,000 opposite-sex couples and by 92,000 same-sex couples (171).

20

Among 29,000,000 teenagers in the country, between 40 percent (156) and 70 percent (113) are reported to be sexually active, and about 1,200,000 teen girls become pregnant each year. Before 1965, 15 percent of teen girls who had babies were unmarried, but by 1983, 37 percent of white girls and 87 percent of Black girls were unwed when giving birth (156). Approximately half of the sexually active teen girls become pregnant in the first six months of that activity, and about 50 percent of the pregnancies are aborted (156).

"Teenage pregnancy is epidemic in the United States and the implication this has on future generations of children cannot be underestimated" (161, p. 163). For example, 82 percent of the girls who give birth at age 15 or younger are the daughters of teenage mothers. More than 1.3 million children live with teen mothers, at least half unmarried, and another 1.6 million live with mothers who were teenagers when the children were born (161).

Teenage girls under 16 who have poor academic skills are five times as likely to become pregnant as those with good achievement (142), and weak students over 16 are two and a half times as likely. The younger the mother at birth, the lower her family income will be. White women giving birth before 17 have mean incomes about half of those who wait until after 20 (142). Children of teen parents score relatively lower academically and are prone to having more emotional problems (142).

Problems in an infant's emotional bonding can occur in either single- or two-parent homes. The Yale Bush Center Infant Care Leave Project (263) reported in 1985 that 85 percent of all women with school-age children have moved into the marketplace, and that nearly half of the married mothers having infants are included. Belsky's (18) research concludes that babies who spend 20 or more hours a week away from parents during their first year face a risk of becoming more unsure than others. Some conclude that no infant should be separated from parents for any significant period of time during the first year of life (161). Bonding breaks can also occur if a child feels abandoned during the second or third years, but after children reach school age, there is a possibility that they may do better when their mothers work (161).

Usually, children from father-present families are better students (207), and in the critical stages when the baby learns trust, either the father or mother may assume major responsibility (29). Among older children, nondelinquents tend to feel they adopted both parents' habits, while delinquents say they loved their mothers most and adopted the mother's ways (7). They feel their fathers should have loved them more (29). Family relations for emotionally disturbed secondary school boys are different, depending on whether fathers are present or absent (250).

21

Strong tensions within families correlate with academic problems and delinquency. A group needing reading assistance in college traced their learning difficulties back to earlier faulty parent-child relationships (210). At earlier levels, when family interactions were less stressful, when agreements and disagreements were explicit and discussions continued until disagreements were settled agreeably, children did not have achievement problems. Families of children having reading difficulties seemed less comfortable with each other (223).

The relationship between home problems and growth is not often simple and direct. For example, delinquent boys from two-parent, disorganized homes had more emotional problems than boys from broken homes with a stable atmosphere (253, 256). Research merely shows tendencies, so one should note that large numbers of youngsters are successful despite home and family problems.

Race and Economics

Race and economic factors probably have less effect on school achievement and delinquency than has been thought. It is true that, although first-graders of all backgrounds enter school with positive anticipation (67), children from high socioeconomic status levels tend toward high achievement, and those from lower socioeconomic levels tend to achieve lower and to have more delinquency (108). Also, the gap between the higher achievers and the lower achievers becomes wider each year (106).

Because the evidence does not support the idea that different races have significantly different academic aptitudes, race does not cause achievement differences. Nor does low income: "low income does not cause reading failure. Rather, low income must be a correlate of factors which do have a causative relationship . . ." (209, p. 2).

To determine the real causes, Clark (43) studied differences between families of high- and low-achieving Black, inner-city children for six months. His major finding was that parents communicated differently with children in families of different achievement levels. In the high-achieving situations, the parents used a "sponsored independence" style. They provided a fairly structured, disciplined home life, developing cohesive family relationships and open communication. They valued education highly, providing diligent support for and supervision of studies, with praise for children's good behavior and school achievement. These parents had upward mobility attitudes, with habits of hard work and delayed gratification. Their children became self-confident and self-disciplined, with middle-class values (43).

The parents of the low-achieving students utilized an "unstructured"

22

communication style. They were usually highly authoritative and very strict or completely the opposite, totally unstructured. They had very loose personal ties with their children, providing no support, guidance, or real assistance with schoolwork. Although they wanted their children to be successful in school, they did not know how to help them (43). So race and money did not affect achievement, but parenting behaviors did.

American families of East Asian descent are noted for being closely knit, and they tend to have high achievement and low rates of delinquency (108). Larger proportions of child delinquency occur among Blacks, Puerto Ricans, Mexicans, and poor whites from rural mountain areas. Statistics show why large numbers of "black children lack self-confidence, feel discouragement, despair, numbness, or rage as they try to grow up on islands of poverty . . . squalid streets with dilapidated housing, crime, and rampant unemployment in a nation of affluence" (108, p. 67). Some Black children do well, however, in learning racial coping strategies (126).

Different languages and dialects also affect the learning. Evidence shows "that SES differences exist during the early school years in children's abilities to utilize semantic and syntactic clues in recalling verbal material . . ." (209, p. 16). In addition, several studies show that beginning readers learn more quickly if reading materials contain vocabulary and sentences patterned in the manner of their local dialects rather than in "standard" English (209). Of course, children of different socioeconomic status do bring different experience backgrounds to school.

Also, among unknown thousands of homeless children sleeping in cars, shelters, and on streets, are an estimated 300,000 "hard-core" homeless runaways and "throwaways" who are abused (113). If they attend school, they will be insecure and will have no place to do assigned homework.

COMMUNITY ENVIRONMENT FACTORS

While no factor causing students to be at risk of failure is entirely a community matter, some are more heavily weighted with community influence than others.

Good Life: Bad Life

After an extensive survey of people whose incomes ranged from very modest to very high, Gallup and Gallup summarized: "The seeds of success, it would seem, are sown not in the soil of riches, but in the good earth of love, understanding, and a nurturing home life" (81, p. 26).

23

Materialistic factors were rated lowest among 12 items people said contributed to their feeling successful. The most important items, with proportions of people choosing them were (1) good health, 58 percent; (2) enjoyable job, 49 percent; (3) happy family, 45 percent; (4) good education, 39 percent; (5) peace of mind, 34 percent; and (6) good friends, 25 percent.

A look at teen life today led the Gallups to say, "Our society appears to have failed to develop an effective and enduring mechanism to communicate sound values and life wisdom from the older generation to the younger" (81, p. 26). A survey of 11,000 eighth- and tenth-graders from a national sample of 200 schools revealed that 26 percent of those in grade 8 and 38 percent in grade 10 had had five or more alcoholic drinks on one occasion during the preceding two weeks (235). One in ten said that they had smoked marijuana and some had used cocaine during the past month.

Accidental injuries are the leading cause of death for young people aged 15 to 25, with 70 percent of the accidents related to automobiles (235). But 56 percent of those surveyed did not regularly wear seatbelts, while 44 percent of tenth-graders and 32 percent of eighth-graders had ridden during the past month with drivers who had used drugs or alcohol. And 64 percent of boys and 19 percent of girls had used a gun during the year (235). Between 10 and 20 percent had attempted suicide. Most eighth- and tenth-graders knew how AIDS is spread and how to use condoms. But they thought AIDS could be prevented by washing and venereal diseases could be prevented with birth control pills (235).

In the inner city, 14 to 25 percent of secondary students fear for their safety. In 1985 about 190 students per 100,000 were assaulted. Attacks on teachers were 8,000 per 100,000 (174). For young Black men, homicide has replaced accidents as the major cause of death, increasing to 66.1 per 100,000 by 1985. It was nearly as high for poor white youths (174).

Life for the 20 to 40 thousand homeless teens on the streets of New York and for approximately 300,000 throughout the country is much more hazardous than for others (113). Most have run away because of stress at home, or have been thrown out because of various reasons including being gay, using drugs, parents' use of drugs, sexual activity, being unloved, being difficult to manage, or parents' lack of money (113).

In cities such as New York, shelters are available for half of the street kids. About 70 percent of those coming to emergency shelters have been severely abused or sexually molested (113). Approximately 60 to 85 percent are depressed, and 25 percent have attempted suicide. Some shelters keep kids for only 15 days, so most must turn to prostitution within a month (113).

Eighty percent of a San Francisco sample were fearful of AIDS, but 25 percent thought it was easily cured. Among army recruits, about 0.15 percent now test positive for the AIDS virus, HIV, but in some big city areas, 0.5 percent to 1.0 percent test postive (113, 115). In a New York sample, 25 percent of street kids in shelters had HIV (113).

Drug and Alcohol Dependence

Alcohol, marijuana, and forms of cocaine are used more frequently by students than other drugs, and the earlier their use is begun the heavier and more serious it becomes (239). The average ages for beginning use of marijuana and alcohol have dropped to 11 and 23 (128). In high schools, about 20 percent drink each day, and another 47 percent drink at various times. About 25 percent use marijuana (128). One in six had tried cocaine (110), with one in 15 using it recently (235).

Experts say four steps usually lead to drug dependence: (1) experimentation, usually with friends; (2) occasional social use; (3) regular use once or twice a week, when the teenager may begin stealing to buy the substance; and (4) dependence, when solitary use occurs almost daily (239).

Narcotics such as heroin have a sedative effect, while drugs classed as depressants can cause intoxication, insomnia, or delirium. Stimulants such as cocaine increase blood pressure, causing short, intense "highs," and become extremely habit forming (239). Hallucinogens such as angel dust distort perception of reality, can cause paranoia and, sometimes, insanity. Marijuana can slow down memory and coordination, while interfering with learning. "Lung damage from smoking 'pot' is estimated to be 17 times greater than that caused by tobacco cigarettes" (239, p. 23). Some of the "designer" drugs, such as "China white," are so potent that they can quickly cause brain damage or death (239). Drugs usually cause crime as users turn to robbery for money needed to support the habit.

Although alcohol can cause dependence and may damage the brain and the liver, drunkenness is common for some teenagers. Of the 10 million alcoholics in this country, an estimated 3.3 million are children.

The serious effects of tobacco smoking in relation to cancer, heart disease, and emphysema are widely known. But young people are less aware that tobacco chewing "can lead to cancer of the lip, cheek, tongue, and throat, causing disfigurement and death" (239, p. 24). While adults have been smoking less, teenagers have been smoking more, with girls smoking more than boys (239).

Drug dependence most often results from peers leading friends to take the first step of experimentation and social use (109, 239). Some also are influenced by parents, and between "12 and 23 million children currently live in homes with an alcoholic parent" (239, p. 24). One of the best predictors of illicit adolescent drug use is the prevalence of drug use and the attitude toward it in the school. Students not committed to academic study are most likely to become drug users (239).

There is a relationship among drug use, school problems, and family difficulties (109, 239). Home communications of drug users often involve much negative, critical communication, inconsistent setting of behavior limits, and unrealistic parental expectations. Students who use drugs do not feel capable, accepted, and valued (131). Nonusers say that their self-respect is more important than pressures to use drugs (239). Drug users often are depressed and they account for much of the recent surge in suicide incidence (109, 168).

Alienated Subcultures

Drug and alcohol abusers tend to feel alienated (239). Children who are inadequate school achievers and those who are poor tend to be unpopular with others and to feel alienated (255). Boys who are poor readers and inept in social skills tend to be accepted only by others like them (169), so they and girls like them form social groups antagonistic toward schools. Even learning disabled students who are receiving good instruction are more positive about school and teachers than continuing, or slower-moving, high school students (21). The feelings of being misfits because of low achievement, poverty, and drug abuse seem to be the roots for the alienated subculture.

Approximately 2,400,000 youths, including about 15 percent of all those from 16 to 19 years of age (163) belong to the subculture, plus more and more younger children now joining this population. They join one of the 600 youth gangs in Los Angeles or hundreds more in New York, Chicago, and other cities. In an early study of gangs, Thrasher (236) said they were a "group originally formed spontaneously and then integrated through conflict," with behavior including "meeting face to face, milling, movement through space as a unit, conflict, and planning" (108, p. 174). In this way they form traditions, solidarity, and attachment to local territory.

In early stages, a gang engages in robbery as a kind of game, which gradually becomes more serious business (108, 211). Gang members recruit others, train them in delinquency, and pull them further into association (108). In addition to the need for protection, youngsters regularly join gangs because they do not see any legitimate opportunities for success through school or employment (108, 212).

26

Social gangs consist of adequately socialized youth who hang out together for companionship because they like each other. Delinquent gangs consist of semisocialized individuals who are fairly emotionally stable, who cooperate in petty thievery, mugging, burglary, and assault to raise "bread." Violent gangs are "primarily organized for emotional gratification, and violence is the theme around which all activities center" (108, p. 189). They build caches of weapons, and regularly engage in gang warfare to enjoy violence and display their power over others. When not fighting other gangs, individuals attempt to prove themselves by "sounding," a pattern of needling, ridiculing, or fighting with other members" (108, p. 189). Through group violence "a disturbed youth may . . . cloak his pathology in the group image, which simultaneously aggrandizes him and lends him anonymity" (108, p. 189).

After a five-year study of criminals, Katz concluded that most crime, like that of violent gangs, is done for thrills and to intimidate and wield power over others (136). Contary to some other researchers, he says the gang leaders are not psychopathic.

Even when no gangs are organized, a counterculture can emerge as lower-class youngsters are faced with middle-class expectations and morality that they reject (253). Such a counterculture has permeated many low socioeconomic communities and schools, especially those populated by minorities. After spending a year visiting schools, Maeroff noted that attendance is atrocious, because there is a culture of cutting. Also, "At school after school, the peer pressure against academic achivement is strong, especially on black males" (159, p. 635). Peer group pressure occurs through negative labeling, exclusion from activities, ostracism, and physical assault (74). Among American Indians, peer and community influences are such that the attitudes of Akwesasne Mohawk students toward school are significantly more favorable if they attend schools off the reservations (167). Sometimes a local leader can make great strides in reversing such attitudes by involving young people in constructive activities (166).

Inadequate Employment Opportunities

If racism disappeared tomorrow, according to Wilson, the problems of minorities of low socioeconomic status would not be solved. Massive energy price increases and other factors causing a slow-down in the U.S. economy have led to unemployment for some groups and a steady deterioration of inner-city neighborhoods and schools (258).

Between 1978 and 1985, the number of manufacturing jobs in the United States declined by 1.7 million, although lower-paying retail jobs increased (154). Since 1979, New York City has lost 600,000 manufacturing jobs and gained 700,000 white-collar clerical jobs (258). But most unemployed young people lack the literacy and social skills needed for white-collar employment. A test battery administered to a national sample of 19- to 23-year-olds in 1980 revealed that the median grade-level scores in reading were 6.8 for Black and 7.5 for Hispanic youths (19). In five of six Oakland high schools, in 1984 the average senior was scoring at the ninth-grade level in math and English (19). One could expect that the young people most likely to be unemployed would score about three or four years lower. When a program was established to train the unemployed in the San Francisco area, one-fifth of the applicants could not read the application form; all the others wrote incoherent paragraphs with spelling and grammatical errors (19). Eight million unemployed in 1982 lacked the literacy skills requisite for on-the-job training (47).

Male teen unemployment dropped in 1986 to 16.3 percent for whites and 39.3 percent for Blacks (264). The expansion of the national economy raised standards for everybody, but the perception of a wide gap between top and bottom incomes creates resentment (66), especially among minorities and the 20 million youth of all races, now aged 16 to 24, who are not likely to attend college (257). Between 1973 and 1986, the proportion of young men aged 20 to 24 who can support a family of three above the poverty level has dropped by one-fourth, from 58.3 percent to 3.8 percent, while the drop among Black males has been more than twice as great. The average real earnings of $9,027 for male workers aged 20 to 24 in 1986 was 25 percent lower than 13 years earlier (257).

Students in special programs have some success, however. Most special needs learners who completed a vocational program in carpentry were successfully employed, even though their employers rated their work as only fair (129). Former LD students from two high schools had faced some unemployment, but most were employed later in service occupations at low wages. They were quite well satisfied and self-reliant (99).

SCHOOL ENVIRONMENT FACTORS

Major school factors that appear to contribute to students becoming at risk are teacher rejection, unfair competition, mass teaching, and low academic performance.

Rejection by Teachers

In decades past, teachers expressed more positive attitudes about middle-class students than those in the lower socioeconomic status (255).

Some teachers have expected pupils who are less esteemed to learn less (247). For example, one group of first-grade teachers believed that the students' social class was the most important factor in predicitng success in learning (93, 255). And when 22 teachers were told a boy shown in a film was learning disabled, while another 22 were told he was normal, their responses after viewing the film showed a different bias in evaluating his filmed performance (58, 75).

When teachers expect low performance, that is what they tend to get. When one group of first-grade teachers believed that girls were better learners than boys, and another group believed both sexes could learn equally well, average achievement of girls was higher in classes whose teacher believed girls were better learners. In the other classes, average achievement for boys and girls was the same (180, 255).

Teachers may treat children in different groups differently. Sometimes the lower groups are given less instructional time. At other times they are given more criticism on minor points, while other groups focus positively on story context (41). Mildly handicapped middle grade students have been found to achieve higher than other mildly handicapped students after their teachers were trained in a teacher expectations program (147).

Teachers sometimes are more critical or expect less achievement of children who speak with a dialect. Cunningham (55) found that 78 percent of teachers would correct dialect miscues in children's oral reading, while only 27 percent would correct nondialect miscues, even though neither type of miscues would affect meaning. Shuy and Frederick (213) found that speech of Black students was rated differently for quality by Black respondents, and middle- and lower-class white respondents.

Labeling

While children often are categorized in various ways during diagnosis of learning difficulties, attaching negative labels to their names can cause teachers to perceive them as inadequate and to expect too little from them (75). Evidence long has shown that labeling a boy as bad tends to make him bad, because "the boy is apt to start seeing himself as others see him and begin acting accordingly or to increase his slightly deviant behavior to where it fits or exceeds his developing poor self-image" (108, p. 147).

Tracking

Dividing the secondary school student body among tracks, or levels according to general achievement, and directing different levels into curricular streams such as college prep, general academic, business, and vocational, is uniformly condemned by researchers. Being held in a low track, regardless of change in motivation, is one of the strongest predictors of delinquency (253), because, "Tracking systems 'lock out' some students and undermine their commitments to education" (37, p. 216).

Counselors sometimes assign students to tracks as much by socioeconomic status as by achievement, and both Black and white students may be discriminated against on that basis (146, 194). In addition, research shows:

> . . . teachers dislike teaching low-ability groups, spend less time preparing for them, and schedule less varied, interesting, and challenging activities for them . . . Instead of being taught via a curriculum or methods specifically suited to their needs, students in low-track classes frequently are not taught much at all or are merely kept quiet with busywork rather than being challenged . . . (89, p. 407)

Other studies (232) indicate that the "students resent their low status and tend to respond defensively by refusing to seriously commit themselves to academic achievement goals and by deriding classmates who do" (89, p. 407). The "excellence movement" calls for schools to reorganize to enhance achievement and eliminate tracking (177, 247).

Low Achievement

As already mentioned, low achievement relates to both dropping out and delinquency, especially for boys (253). One researcher matched 76 male and 52 female elementary students under court supervision with equivalent students in the general population. Records showed court-supervised girls had more unstable home conditions and were older than classmates, while boys had low achievement and poor attitudes and work habits (108). Taglianetti (234) found failure to read caused school failure and contributed to delinquency.

Boys with low achievement are twice as prone to delinquent behavior as those with good grades, and those with poor achievement and delinquent friends are four times as likely to become delinquent (253). This seems to be an attempt to appear successful in one way in the eyes of friends (253). The amount of stress low achievment causes is apparent, because after boys drop out of school, there is a marked drop in the amount of delinquent behavior (158, 253). Currently, 13 to 24 percent drop out, with 50 percent or more dropping out in some large cities (100). But far more left school early 10 to 20 years ago (264).

Unfair Competition in Graded Schools

Graded schools, organized since about 1840 so that students of one age are all expected to learn and achieve at exactly the same level, are certain to cause some students to feel so highly frustrated that they either become very emotionally disturbed or very aggressive (203, 48). As noted earlier, intelligence explains about 70 percent of variability in learning, and when the best individual tests are used, they show a very wide range of academic aptitude in every class. Cook and Clymer say:

> When intelligence is measured and converted into age units, the range among first-graders (6-year-olds) is 4 years. At the seventh-grade level (12-year-olds), the range is 8 years. The typical range of ability in any grade (disregarding the 2 percent of pupils at each end of the distribution) is equal to two-thirds of the chronological age of the median pupil in that grade.

> When achievement in the various subjects is measured at each grade level, the range of achievement is found to be approximately the same as that for intelligence as described above. (48, pp. 206-7)

Karweit explained that in a typical fifth-grade class, students will be achieving at third, fourth, fifth, sixth, and seventh-grade levels (135, p. 85). This spread in achievement grows wider each year (48), unless the work is geared only to the lowest level of students. Obviously, about a third or a fourth of the students do not have the academic aptitudes needed to succeed with the average students. Because they soon recognize that they cannot succeed in competing academically, they, as noted earlier, develop inadequate self-images, or they try to protect their egos by finding something in which they can compete successfully—disruptive and delinquent behavior (149). Even some of the most talented resort to disruption when overly bored. Consequently, in analyzing evidence on the causes of delinquency, Schafer and Polk (206) concluded that the primary factor is the inflexible, competitive structure of the schools.

31

Chapter 3

IMMEDIATE STEPS WITH STUDENTS AT RISK

Research indicates that procedures most successful with students at risk are largely the same as those successful with other students. More highly motivated students are able to cope, even when the best types of teaching are not utilized.

IDENTIFICATION OF STUDENTS AT RISK

Not every kindergarten screening scale is always predictive of success (206), but some are more so than others (51). Later, a combination of sixth-grade achievement scores and eighth-grade aptitude scores predict senior high school passage of minimum competency examinations with 80 percent accuracy (26). At the time that they are hoping to enter college, students' estimates of their own reading ability, however, have little relation to reality (191).

Future aggressive behavior of residential school students can be predicted by observation of behavior traits (96), and among Black urban first-graders the single best predictor of future delinquency is being an "angry loner," both shy and aggressive (123). (Others say hyperactivity is the best predictor.)

Learning style inventories are helpful in identifying needs (187). And self-concepts can be estimated by having children complete a set of incomplete statements showing their feelings about a number of school and family matters (27). Some traits suggesting serious emotional problems and antisocial personality disorders have been listed earlier. And a teacher should be concerned about a child rejected by others (42).

Because of conflicting descriptions, teachers often request help in screening for children having learning disabilities. Sartain and Seamen (204) asked a teacher and two student teachers in several classrooms to check behaviors of children. Three observers who had worked with children for a month or more agreed closely on children's traits. In comparing findings with results of psychologists' diagnoses, they concluded that a child probably suffered from learning disability if he or she exhibited *seven* of the traits. One, two, or three of such behaviors are quite normal. The list of symptomatic traits follows:

Emotional Symptoms

_____ Is constantly inattentive
_____ Is easily distracted
_____ Is easily frustrated
_____ Is very impulsive (reckless)
_____ Touches, clings to others excessively
_____ Refuses to speak to teacher, group
_____ Is withdrawn, shy
_____ Is unusually aggressive
_____ Has frequent rage reactions, tantrums
_____ Is overexcitable in normal play
_____ Is inconsistent in relationships
_____ Adjusts poorly to change
_____ Stutters or often stammers
_____ Has jerky, explosive speech

Perceptual Symptoms

_____ Cannot organize work, materials
_____ Is unable to follow directions
_____ Exhibits thought perseveration (repeats idea involuntarily)
_____ Is often unable to discriminate differences in size, shape
_____ Is often unable to discriminate figure from ground
_____ Is often unable to copy letters or geometric figures
_____ Is often unable to discriminate a part from the whole
_____ Is often unable to judge distance
_____ Is often unable to discriminate through sense of touch
_____ Reverses letters, numbers, words

Motor Symptoms

_____ Writes, prints, draws poorly
_____ Hands tremble or jerk
_____ Is generally clumsy, awkward
_____ Is hyperactive (overactive, restless)
_____ Is hypoactive (listless, lethargic)
_____ Eyeballs oscillate rapidly, involuntarily
_____ Is unable to direct both eyes to the same object
_____ Exhibits motor perseveration (difficulty ceasing repetition of a movement)

Other Symptoms

_____ Is unable to speak
_____ Has mild speech irregularities

_____ Is physically immature for age
_____ Is physically advanced for age
_____ Is unable to translate thoughts from speech to writing
_____ Quickly forgets spelling after written practice
_____ Is unable to explain idea after hearing example
_____ Is unable to recall sequence of events after listening to story
_____ Quickly forgets sight vocabulary that seemed thoroughly learned
_____ Quickly forgets word analysis techniques
_____ Is unable to explain sentences he/she reads aloud
_____ Has special difficulty in learning arithmetic

Whenever possible, a teacher's tentative decision about a student's serious needs should be double-checked with a psychologist or other specialist.

REFERRAL TO SPECIALISTS

Public Law 94-142 requires every special student to be diagnosed and taught in the least restrictive environment using a plan designed by teacher, parent, and specialist. Teachers have learned to adapt to the needs of special students who are mainstreamed (182), and "normal" children learn to be helpful to such children (101). Reading and speech specialists also can be helpful in diagnosis and planning (106). In addition, psychologists and psychiatrists are having some success in treating problems of school phobia, depression, hyperactivity, and antisocial aggressiveness through procedures such as coaching, behavior modification, and cognitive therapy (122, 225, 254).

CARING AND MENTORING

Teacher commitment to improve students' academic and social performance, as measured by student perceptions that teachers care, has been established as a significant variable in climates of excellent schools (12, 60, 252). When one visits such schools, one sees that the level of caring is most striking (155). It requires getting to know the child personally through sympathetic individual diagnostic procedures such as the individual reading inventory (106), and also requires developing an understanding, supportive rapport (24).

Knowing the child well helps one to notice possibilities of learning disabilities and to determine what will work best in teaching (141). One individualized technique, the impress method, provides multisensory input for learning disabled students and others having special learning styles. The child having reading difficulty reads material visually while listening to a tape or to the teacher reading the same material aloud. It sometimes produces exceptional gains (120). A keyword mnemonic technique also has been used successfully in helping learning disabled children to remember (165).

Mentoring, a friendly, personal, supportive, instructive relationship between an adult and a student, is particularly beneficial in promoting achievement (155), and in counteracting some antisocial personality disorders (161). In this, as in all teaching, it is essential to recognize that every child in school can learn (247), although in different ways and at different rates. Through patient, individual attention in and outside of school, teachers, aides, or well-chosen volunteers can develop a productive mentoring relationship that may save a student at risk.

PROVIDING INDIVIDUAL SUCCESS THROUGH ADAPTED INSTRUCTION

The most successful teachers usually combine whole-class work on general concept development with flexible small-group work on the skills of communication and math (73, 247). Whole-class instruction is particularly ineffective for students at risk (130, 186), and students pay better attention in small groups (98, 135). Although no particular system of organization for differentiated instruction has been found to be consistently most successful (179), schools having exceptional success invariably provide some form of individualization (155, 247).

Achievement is highest when teachers base their planning on ongoing diagnosis (199). One approach is for a teacher to begin a class with general instruction and an assignment, or with independent project work. Small groups then can be pulled aside for 10-15 minutes at a time to work at their own level on a skill related to the unit under study, or to learn something through a particular learning style. By meeting with each small group a couple of times a week, the teacher can reduce pupils' stress (181), adjust work to levels that will guarantee success, and overcome learning apathy (189). Self-esteem grows if the teacher provides frequent feedback for accomplishments (138, 228).

While some question the need to consider individual learning styles in differentiated teaching (89), Dunn has found that "achieving youngsters invariably exhibit learning styles that differ from underachieving ones" (61, p. 144). Learning disabled students seem to be more impulsive than reflective in style, and more dependent than others on environmental clues (22). Learning disabled students' preferences of perceptual modalities, from most to least, are kinesthetic, tactual, auditory, and visual

35

(116), but those having high visual preference have made significant gains with a tactual-kinesthetic treatment (116).

Carbo found that some youngsters develop an intuitive awareness of word patterns instead of an analytic perception, so those having difficulty with phonics sometimes are global learners who will learn much better through listening to tapes while reading the story, through writing, and through other meaningful approaches (35).

COOPERATIVE LEARNING

Cooperative learning (127) and the variation called Team-Assisted Individualization (216) are particularly effective in differentiating instruction (89, 148). They are especially suitable for use with children at risk because children of different backgrounds and abilities are mixed together in small, temporary groups. Each group is given the same or different problems to solve, with children working individually and cooperatively until everybody in the group agrees on the response. Problems may be as simple as constructing a better sentence or as complex as writing an essay, working a set of math problems, or planning a science experiment, as well as using educational games (89).

By rewarding both indivdual and group achievement, teachers can counteract the statement that "Our society is filled with alienated children . . ., yet within schools competitive and individualistic efforts are emphasized, where students are isolated from and pitted against each other. . ." (127, p. 123).

Cooperative learning combines fun and lively interaction (188) and develops a sense of belonging (95), while being used suitably in a number of fields of study (218, 241, 261).

RECOGNIZING AND REWARDING PROGRESS

Sincere praise and other nominal rewards are needed, particularly to raise the self-concepts and motivate children at risk (153, 214). In superior schools, academic awards are given and a large proportion of students receive awards at various times (247).

STRONG PROGRAMS ON SUBSTANCE DEPENDENCY

Although they are not always successful, strong programs on drug and alcohol dependency are desperately needed (239). The effectiveness of programs to reduce adult smoking suggests that health education in other areas may be equally effective with time.

Chapter 4

PARENT INVOLVEMENT IN PREVENTING STUDENT PROBLEMS

During the first twelve years of schooling, parents have a great amount of control over 87 percent of a student's waking time (243). And activities related to home life are more important than both socioeconomic status and school functions in the child's development (153, 243). One psychologist who monitored treatment of 250 families with antisocial children concluded that most delinquency may develop because of ineffective parenting skills (123).

HOME FACTORS AFFECTING STUDENT ACHIEVEMENT

An examination of working-class family parenting of very successful and nonsuccessful high school students showed parents of successful students emphasized vigilant parenting, strong family orientation, and expectation of good school achievement. They emphasized family responsibility first, supported study efforts, and used religion to counterbalance negative community influences (236).

Research reveals many family factors that affect student achievement: mother's use of the library, number of books and good magazines in the home, father's employment in professional or skilled work, visits to museums and places of interest, parents' discussion with children of news and books read, attendance by parents at school functions, levels of parents' education, and attitudes of parents toward education (143, 201). Social comfort at home is beneficial, while emotional conflict defeats concentration on study and memory (201). Parental example counts, because, as already noted, more children of criminal parents than of noncriminal parents become delinquent, and more daughters of unmarried mothers than married mothers become pregnant during teen years.

PARENTS AND TEACHERS

Visits of teachers to homes, very helpful and previously required in some schools, are done now by only 2 percent of teachers (153). But more teachers schedule parent conferences regularly to discuss school curriculum and the child's progress (69).

37

Wayson's team found that excellent schools provide services to parents such as lectures, use of facilities, and community projects (247). They also involve parents as volunteers in reading with children, coaching dramatics, making lab presentations, and acting as mentors (247). They use a variety of ways to communicate school programs to parents, including graphic progress reports, classroom visits, and displays of student work (247). Some teachers have developed their communication skills so well that they have better access than others to parents for collaborative work (89).

PARENT TRAINING

Many parents seem to need advice and encouragement from the school (217). Parent training programs have been used fairly often, and about two-thirds or more of these programs produce better student performance (201). In an example of one that did not work, training was conducted through individual home visits (83).

Use of a pretraining needs questionnaire, followed later with open-ended discussions, has been effective in planning training for parents of preschool children (245). Very concrete suggestions were found much better than theoretical presentations in working with Mexican-American parents (160).

Parent training in family problem solving, crisis management, and monitoring and rewarding behavior has resulted in sharply improved student performance (123). Ten weekly library experiences with inner-city parents and children, plus 220 suggestions for home language experiences, resulted in significant language gains for 15 involved families in comparison with noninvolved families (233). When parents were encouraged to take children just completing first grade to the library weekly during the summer, their reading achievement at the beginning of second grade was far superior to that of those who had not been taken to the library (220). And studies with children aged 6 to 13 revealed that paired reading, parent and child reading together regularly, resulted in 3 to 5 times the normal growth in reading achievement (237). Excellent ideas for parent training are summarized in these works in the Bibliography: 71, 107, 111, 121.

Chapter 5

LONG-TERM PREVENTION PLANNING

To some boys and girls, the school is an intolerable place where they have faced many impossible tasks and unsympathetic adults.

The failure of the school to respond to individual human and academic needs of children has contributed greatly to children being at risk, and "so long as that failure persists, delinquency, as well as other school-related problems, will persist" (146, p. 232).

CALLS TO EXCELLENCE

It seems appropriate to examine a sample of the numerous presentations on school reform published during the 1980s to see whether they offer solutions for children at risk. The one receiving the most attention, *A Nation At Risk*, offered little for such youngsters. It recommended increasing the number of required academic courses in high schools, more rigorous textbooks, student discipline codes that would make more efficient use of class time, longer school days and years, grouping and promotion of students according to progress rather than chronological age, improved incentives for teachers, and other changes (173).

Action for Excellence: A Comprehensive Plan to Improve Our Nation's Schools recommended upgraded skills instruction, increased problem solving, reduced electives, upgrading textbooks, use of computers, and more rigorously trained teachers (1). *The Failure of Our Public Schools: The Causes and a Solution* called for funding schools on the basis of academic achievement instead of attendance (68). *Education and Economic Progress: Toward a National Educational Policy: The Federal Role* called for federal legislation to stress mathematics and science, with foreign language and higher skills for students of high aptitudes (63). The three *Paideia Proposals* stressed early admission to school, strong academic standards, a few extracurricular activities to develop character, and some limited vocational introduction activities (2, 3, 4).

Because people on the commissions and committees making these recommendations were politicians, business men, and university leaders with little apparent knowledge of children's learning problems, their recommendations were directed largely at the upper third of the student body, with scant concern for students at risk. Because of their suggestions, however, many departments of education have mandated increased requirements in academic fields for high school graduation. Some districts also have required more homework assignments at all levels, with little consideration for its quality, and no consideration for the problems of the many students who have jobs or no privacy for study. These practices, insensitive to difficulties of at least one-third of the students, can only increase their frustrations (262), risking increased delinquency, dropouts, and suicides.

Better Suggestions

Fortunately, more useful suggestions have been offered in studies by Goodlad (91) and Boyer (28), who display knowledge of psychology and human development. Goodlad's eight-year examination of schools, detailed in *A Place Called School: Prospects for the Future*, mentioned concern about the passiveness in students and the rather traditional style of teaching. He recommended a balanced academic curriculum, and of importance to teachers of students at risk, said that if one instructional method does not work with a child, others should be tried. He advised early admission to schools where teachers would humanize knowledge to make learning less abstract. And he would avoid inflexible, ability-level tracking, organizing schools, instead, in a nongraded, continuous progress manner to accept human differences and support differentiated development.

Boyer's book, *High School: A Report on Secondary Education in America*, was based on a two-year study of 15 schools and funded by the Carnegie Foundation for the Advancement of Teaching. He recommends strong studies in usual academic areas, plus work in the arts, health, technology, and introductory vocational education. He would offer a core curriculum with one-third of the time remaining for electives to meet individual needs and interests. Of importance for children at risk, he advises close relationships between students and counselors or teachers who are trusted by students. He also would identify failure patterns early and provide alternative programs, where students would attain a feeling of belonging while working toward a reasonably high standard.

Felt (70) described a number of the excellence studies, and Wayson et al. (247) summarized them and added findings related to one hundred excellent schools throughout the country. These and other studies will be considered in further suggestions for preventing student problems.

EARLY CHILDHOOD PROGRAMS

For every dollar spent on preschool education of disadvantaged children, an estimated $4.75 will be saved in later social services (190). Numerous studies clarify the value of preschool preparation. In a review of programs for 3- and 4-year-olds, researchers found that children who participated in the experimental programs, had, in later years, better grades, fewer failures, fewer absences, and greater self-esteem than those who were not involved (230). When curricula provided for child-initiated learning, later grades were not higher, but at age 15, fewer students had been involved in delinquent behaviors (230).

Children, mostly Black minority, who had been in a preschool program, had higher reading scores than equivalent groups in grades 1, 2, and 3, and sometimes their behavior was significantly better (85). About half of 123 "disadvantaged" children in a low-socioeconomic area were involved in a high-quality preschool program, while the others were not. Twenty-two years later, 51 percent of the nonpreschool individuals had been detained and arrested, while only 31 percent of those having preschool experience had been detained and arrested (123).

Therapeutic programs seem valuable, too. Ninety-four children from a therapeutic nursery program for the emotionally disturbed had adjusted well enough so that teachers five years later rated their behavior as highly as that of others (64). After being identified as low achievers in a kindergarten screening, 30 children given extra readiness experiences two afternoons a week achieved at higher levels than high-risk students not having the program in previous years (102). Children reading and participating in extra experiences in a transitional first grade were rated as significantly better in relation to conduct disorders, attention problems, anxiety withdrawal, and motor excess, than children who needed but did not enroll in the transitional program (33).

In a meta-analysis of 74 studies, Casto and Mastropieri concluded that early intervention with handicapped populations produces a sizable positive effect, and that longer intensive programs were most efficacious (38). Their findings that the length of parent involvement and the age of entry into the program might not be statistically important, were hotly criticized by others (62, 229), then rebutted by the original researchers (39, 40).

Although Head Start reaches only 16 percent of those who need it (34), since 1980, 21 states have increased spending for prekindergartens and five have begun contributing to Head Start (133). Favorable long-term effects for kindergarten work have prompted increasing programs for 4-years-olds (76). Great care must be taken, however, to involve them in activity at their maturation levels (249), instead of making them feel stress from overdemanding academically oriented, worksheet activities (65, 76).

HUMANIZING SCHOOLS TO MEET INDIVIDUAL NEEDS

The dehumanizing effects of large, impersonal classes in large, regimented schools is detrimental to personal development and conducive to stress and alienation (146, 253). Quick-fix "improvements" in the past have not given adequate consideration to the complexity of the problems (90, p. 87).

Curriculum for Continuous Individual Progress

Laypeople's lack of knowledge of how children learn threatens the bottom half of student populations when pressures are exerted to maintain curriculum geared to the entrenched, graded, unit-age system (6). A multiple regression study shows that the average aptitude of groups is the main determinant of content coverage (15). Studies suggest that the easiest way to increase achievement is to increase the pace of instruction, but this diminishes rather than enhances learning for those with lowest readiness (15).

An analysis of instructional plans suggests "that the emphasis should be on maximizing each student's achievement, even if this should mean maintaining or even increasing the range of individual differences in achievement levels" (89, p. 358). One reason research has not always shown differentiated instruction plans to produce better results is that they often are not fully initiated (89). Also, data limited to achievement test score averages does not detect values to individuals at risk.

Jones's (132) classic experiment clearly demonstrated the value of differentiated teaching over a single-level curriculum. And "more recent evaluations of programs classified as 'adaptive education' have shown more positive results..." (89, p. 364). A twenty-year demonstration of nongraded education at Falk School, University of Pittsburgh, has not only produced excellent achievement, but also a reduction in the amount of psychiatric counseling needed by students having problems upon entry (69). In another situation, the work of 70 special education students in an individualized program was determined by analysis of variance to be significantly higher than that of other students not involved in individualization (32).

In Wayson's study, excellent schools have curriculum by faculty for a program that is not rigid and lock-step, but includes differentiated grouping and enrichment (247). Research indicates that some students spend twice as much time on task and complete three times as much work when permitted to work at their own pace in an individualized program (244). Such a program also is conducive to developing positive attitudes (244). In observing excellent schools, Lipsitz noted that they insist on common humanity of their inhabitants, and one striking feature "is their willingness and ability to adapt all school practices to the individual differences in intellectual, biological, and social maturation of their students" (155).

No More Assembly Lines Inside Schools

Evidence reviewed so far shows that the lock-step, graded-school organization introduced in the United States in about 1840, has caused distress, impaired egos, anger, depression, suicides, delinquency, and dropouts among one-fourth to one-third of students. In what better ways can the continuous, differentiated curriculum be delivered in schools?

While most schools today are not very adaptive (59), students who might be at risk do best in structures that encourage small-group/whole-class instruction (89, 251). Lowest-ability children do best when placed in high-achieving schools (89), and in the multiability classroom they have increased opportunities for academic participation and success (45). In mixed-ability grouping, similar in some ways to cooperative learning, there are no low-status groups. In-service education experimentation shows teachers learn to involve students in a richer range of activities for mixed-ability work (45).

Organization for complete one-to-one teaching is not recommended, because a teacher cannot spend enough time with each pupil (195, 203) and because some systems prevent student interaction and thinking by extensive use of packaged materials (89). While many faults can be found with grouping (94), it provides more time for direct instruction (203), and produces strong achievement. In one superior situation, "The most salient dimension in second-grade classes appeared to be flexibility of grouping... The teachers would regroup students according to needs..." (73, p. 25). "For Grade Five classes, the same dimension appeared" (73, p. 25).

Flexible grouping fits with a nongraded school organization, which was found effective years ago by Hillson (117), by Ingram (124), and by Skapski (215). Nongrading has been tried a bit in many places (176), and long has been demonstrated to be very effective at the University of Pittsburgh (69). More individualized and small-group work occurs in schools that label themselves nongraded than in other schools (164).

When those schools doing a poor job of implementing differentiated instruction are eliminated from the comparison, individualized instruction proves more effective than traditional programs (89).

In order to get to know students well and differentiate teaching, an effective procedure used at both elementary and secondary levels is to assign a team of three or four instructors to the same group of students for several years (178). The grouping within classes that can then be done has advantages over homogeneous sectioning because of its flexibility in use of time and in shifting group membership (89, 203). Within-class grouping has been found beneficial, particularly in reading (15) and mathematics (89, 216). Another successful secondary school procedure for knowing children better is to have homeroom teachers teaching double subjects such as math and science. Felt says, ''. . . it is better for one teacher to teach 80 students both English and history than one teacher to teach 160 students. . .'' (70, p. 200). In one excellent junior high school that permitted students to select their own advisers and meet with them weekly, attendance rose from 88 percent to 93 percent within two years and the dropout rate decreased by two-thirds (247).

An inspiring step toward ridding schools of Henry Ford's assembly line has been taken in Ohio's Classroom of the Future "where the heart of the system is knowing the individual student" (178). Open from 7:00 a.m. to 7:00 p.m., it covers preschool through grade 12, plus vocational education for adults. The second daily shift of staff includes coaches, music and dance teachers, scout leaders, and so on, making it possible for students to stay the full day while their parents are at work (178).

The plan calls for children to enter school on their fifth birthday, as they do in New Zealand and some other countries. This forces faculty to recognize each learner as an individual and to move him or her into appropriate groups gradually. Teachers work in small teams with the same set of mixed-age children for several years so that learning can be highly adapted and personalized. The structure includes four-year spans for elementary, middle, and high school years. Groups are racially integrated, and faculty planning covers procedures to prevent any children from becoming at risk (178).

Progress reported after the first couple of years is positive, and more exact evaluation will be provided at the end of the first five years.

Choices for Living

Pull-out programs to give brief assistance to students at risk may penalize children because of class work they miss through coordination problems (78). The long-term, pull-out procedure for Pennsylvania's

Commonwealth Classroom, however, is producing results (9). Students who are at risk because of uncooperative behavior and poor study habits are placed in several rooms in a minischool within the regular school. There, specially selected teachers offer the regular school subjects, while also incorporating a "School Survival Skills Curriculum," which stresses self-monitoring on participation habits and how to keep on task. Students work in the Commonwealth Classrooms for ten weeks to a year or more, while trying to prove that they have learned the survival skills (9). Even after returning to regular rooms, they periodically report back to Commonwealth teachers before morning classes for reassessment of their habits of self-responsibility (9). For most students, experience in the Commonwealth classrooms results in improved attendance and an improvement in grades (9).

Noncollege-bound students are especially concerned about employment, so they will be interested in education only when schools learn ways to "engage students of all backgrounds and all ability levels, . . . persuade them that the enterprise is worthwhile, and respond to their individual needs in a fashion that will enable them to succeed" (227, p. 78). Magnet schools seem to help, as shown by good behavior and lower dropout rates (23). Vocational-technical high schools also have often been quite successful.

CHARACTER AND CULTURAL DEVELOPMENT

Personal development is essential to prevent students becoming at risk. Among beginning teachers, 80 percent believe values and character development should be taught (103), while 62 percent of parents feel character educational material should be suited to the community (80). Seventy-two percent of parents favor sex education in high school and 52 percent want it in elementary school (80).

Multicultural Instruction

Commitment to multicultural education has several values (54), one of which is reducing violence (25). Children's extended discussions of human merit, needs, and so forth, lead them to prefer equality (151). Different ethnic groups have their own values (145, 221), which can be shared and understood through multicultural education programs. Extensive suggestions on multicultural education are available (14, 87).

45

Personal Development

Opinions differ completely on the values of outdoor survival experiences in treating antisocial behavior (84). In a brief set of camp activities where data were collected carefully, Kay (137) found that after 6-day experiences, postcamp moral judgments had not changed on the average, but students who participated most vigorously were most influenced (137). In a four-year study of 700 boys in weekly field trips, sports, other activities, and group therapy, Feldman found that antisocial boys grouped with other antisocial boys did not improve. But when antisocial boys were mixed in groups of largely prosocial boys, 91 percent of them reduced their antisocial behavior by 50 percent (123). Satterfield determined that untreated hyperactive children were 10 to 20 times more likely to become delinquent than those given multimodal treatments (123).

Reward systems are very helpful in changing behavior, but having socially disturbed students select the system is not particularly beneficial (13). The teacher's guidance in goal-setting, however, constantly is shown to contribute to good behavior and achievement (11, 77, 192). And in evaluating the excellent progress of the lowest quarter of students in three middle schools and two high schools, Klausmeier (144) concluded that the implementation of goal-setting strategy appeared to be the determining factor in producing consistently higher student achievement.

CONCLUSION—A CALL TO ACTION

The data about today's children and youth are as chilling as the sound of the fire siren blasting to stop at the house next door.

The facts speak for themselves.

"One-third of the 40 million school-aged children in the United States are at risk of either failing, dropping out, or falling victim to crime, drugs, teenaged pregnancy, or chronic unemployment.... For every two children we educate, we lose one, and the consequences are disastrous" (183).

In one typical year recently, 1,500,000 young people were arrested for juvenile crimes, even though police usually pick up only about one-fifth of those they apprehend while committing illegal acts (158).

"If you teach high school, the chances are that about one-fourth of the students in your classes regularly smoke marijuana, more than two-thirds regularly use alcohol, and approximately one-fifth drink on a daily basis" (239, p. 18).

The suicide rate among young people tripled during the last 25 yearts (184). Every hour of every day, 57 teenagers attempt suicide, making well over 1,000 attempts a day. Eighteen of these attempts succeed daily (181).

Approximately 1,200,000 teenage girls become pregnant each year. About 1,540 give birth to a baby each day (100).

One million illiterates a year are coming through the schools—850,000 as dropouts and 150,000 as pushouts (105).

Researchers believe that six out of ten students cannot understand what they read in the newspaper (30).

BIBLIOGRAPHY

1. *Action for Excellence: A Comprehensive Plan to Improve Our Nation's Schools.* Denver: Education Commission of the States, 1983.

2. Adler, Mortimer J. *The Paideia Program.* New York: Macmillan, 1984.

3. _____. *Paideia Problems and Possibilities: A Consideration of Questions Raised by the Paideia Proposal.* New York: Macmillan, 1983.

4. _____. *The Paideia Proposal: An Educational Manifesto.* New York: Macmillan, 1982.

5. Andera, Frank, and Atwell, Beverly. "Understanding the Learning Styles of the Native-American Student." *The Balance Sheet* (March/April 1988): 13-14.

6. Anderson, Robert H. "Political Pressures on Supervisor." In *Critical Issues in Curriculum*, edited by L. N. Tanner, 60-82. Chicago: National Society for the Study of Education, University of Chicago Press, 1988.

7. Andry, Robert G. *Delinquency and Parental Pathology.* London: Staples, 1971.

8. Anthony, Barbara J. H. "A Study of Congruence between Learning Style Preference and Teaching Style Preference, Student Attitudes, and Achievement among Fifth-grade Students." Ph.D. diss., University of Alabama, 1984.

9. "Arsenal Commonwealth Classroom: A Beneficial Alternative." Pittsburgh: Pittsburgh Board of Education, 1988.

10. Atman, Kathryn S., and Hanna, James W. "Conation, Goal Accomplishment Style, and Academic Achievement at the Middle School Level." *Research Annual 1987: Selected Studies*, 19-35. Columbus, Ohio: National Middle School Association, 1987.

11. Atman, Kathryn S., and Santillo, Richard. "Conative Processes and Goal Accomplishment Style of Junior High School Students." Paper presented at American Educational Research Association, New Orleans, Louisiana, April 8, 1988.

12. Austin, Gilbert R., and Garber, Herbert. *Research on Exemplary Schools.* Orlando, Fla.: Academic Press, 1985.

13. Bair, Sheryl J. "Effects of Involvement in Reward Selection on Intrinsic Motivation of Severe Behavior Handicapped Students." Ph.D. diss., Kent State University, 1987.

14. Banks, James A. *Multiethnic Education: Theory and Practice.* Boston: Allyn and Bacon, 1988.

15. Barr, Rebecca. "Classroom Reading Instruction from a Sociological Perspective." *Journal of Reading Behavior* 14, no. 4 (1982): 375-89.

16. *Barriers to Excellence: Our Children at Risk.* Boston: National Coalition of Advocates for Students, 1985.

17. Beentjes, Johannes W. J., and Van der Voort, Tom H. A. "Television's Impact on Children's Reading Skills: A Review of Research." *Reading Research Quarterly* 23, no. 4 (Fall 1988): 389-413.

18. Belsky, J. "Infant Day Care: A Cause for Concern?" *Zero to Three* 6, no. 5 (September 1986), Bulletin of the National Center for Clinical Infant Programs, Washington, D.C.

19. Bernick, M. "Illiteracy and Inner-City Unemployment." *Phi Delta Kappan* 67, no. 5 (January 1986): 364-67.

20. Bierman, K. L. "Cognitive Development and Clinical Interviews with Children." In *Advances in Clinical and Child Psychology*, edited by B. B. Lahey and A. E. Kazdin, 217-50. New York: Plenum, 1983.

21. Blackaller, Carrie A. S. "Alienation Attitudes of Learning Disabled, Continuation, and Academicaly Average High School Students." Ph.D. diss., University of Southern California, 1988.

22. Blackman, Sheldon, and Goldstein, Kenneth M. "Cognitive Styles and Learning Disabilities." *Journal of Learning Disabilities* 15, no. 2 (February 1982): 106-15.

23. Blank, Rolf K. "Effects of Magnet Schools on the Quality of Education in Urban Districts." *Phi Delta Kappan* 66, no. 4 (December 1984): 270-72.

24. Boesel, D., et al. *Violent Schools—Safe Schools.* National Institute of Education. Washington, D.C.: U.S. Government Printing Office, 1978.

25. Booth, Terry L. "The Schooling of Child-Normative Violence." Ph.D. diss., University of Kansas, 1987.

26. Bostic, Jeff Q., et al. "A Method for Early Identification of Students Likely to Fail in a Minimum Competency Exit Level Test: Early Prediction of Scores on the Texas Educational Assessment of Minimum Skills (TEAMS)." Paper presented at Association of Teacher Educators, Houston, Texas, February 14-18, 1987. Ed 281 893.

27. Bourisseau, Whitfield. "To Fathom the Self: Appraisal in School." In *The Child and His Image*, edited by Kaoru Yamamoto, 80-120. Boston: Houghton Mifflin, 1972.

28. Boyer, Ernest L. *High School: A Report on Secondary Education in America.* New York: Harper & Row, 1983.

29. Brazelton, T. B. *Working and Caring.* Reading, Mass.: Addison-Wesley, 1985.

30. Brennan, Michael. "Students Fail in Using School Skills to Solve Problems of Everyday Life." *Pittsburgh Press*, February 15, 1989.

31. Brower, M. "Gang Violence: Color It Real." *People Weekly* 129 (2 May 1988): 42-47.

32. Burns, Danny L. "Relationship between Individual Educational Programs and Achievement Test Scores of Exceptional Children." Ph.D. diss., University of Alabama, 1984.

33. Caggiano, John A. "A Study of the Effectiveness of Transitional First Grade in a Suburban School District." Ph.D. diss., Temple University, 1984.

34. *Call for Action to Make Our Nation Safe for Children: A Briefing Book on the Status of American Children in 1988*. Washington, D.C.: Children's Defense Fund, 1988.

35. Carbo, Marie. "Reading Styles Research: 'What Works' Isn't Always Phonics." *Phi Delta Kappan* 68, no. 6 (February 1987): 431-35.

36. _____. "Reading Styles: Key to Preventing Reading Failure." *Student Learning Styles and Brain Behavior*, 126-35. Reston, Va.: National Association of Secondary School Principals, 1982.

37. Carey, James T., and McAnany, Patrick D. *Introduction to Juvenile Delinquency: Youth and the Law*. Englewood Cliffs, N.J.: Prentice-Hall, 1984.

38. Casto, Glendon, and Mastropieri, Margo A. "The Efficacy of Early Intervention Programs: A Meta-Analysis." *Exceptional Children* 52, no. 5 (February 1986): 417-24.

39. _____. "Much Ado About Nothing: A Reply to Dunst and Snyder." *Exceptional Children* 53, no. 3 (November 1986): 277-79.

40. _____. "Strain and Smith Do Protest Too Much: A Response." *Exceptional Children* 53, no. 3 (November 1986): 266-68.

41. Cazden, Courtney B. "Contexts for Literacy: In the Mind and in the Classroom." *Journal of Reading Behavior* 14, no. 4 (1982): 413-27.

42. Chance, Paul. "Kids without Friends." *Psychology Today* 23, no. 1/2 (January/February 1989): 29-31.

43. Clark, Reginald M. *Family Life and School Achievement: Why Poor Black Children Succeed or Fail*. Chicago: University of Chicago Press, 1984.

44. Cline, F. *Understanding and Treating the Severely Disturbed Child*. Evergreen, Colo.: Evergreen Consultants in Human Behavior, 1979.

45. Cohen, Elizabeth G. "A Multi-Ability Approach to the Integrated Classroom." *Journal of Reading Behavior* 14, no. 4 (1982): 439-60.

46. Collier, James L. "What Your Child Fears Most." *Reader's Digest*, August 1988, 7-12.

47. *Common Focus: An Exchange of Information about Early Adolescence*. Center for Early Adolescent Studies and Adolescent Literacy, University of North Carolina, 1986, 7, 1.

48. Cook, Walter W., and Clymer, Theodore. "Acceleration and Retardation." In *Individualizing Instruction*, edited by Nelson B. Henry, 177-

208. Chicago: National Society for the Study of Education, University of Chicago Press, 1962.

49. Cook, W. D. *Adult Literacy in the U.S.* Newark, Del.: International Reading Association, 1977.

50. Cooks, Helen C. "The Black High School Student: Post-secondary Aspirations, Expectations, Plans, and Perceived Opportunity Options." Ph.D. diss., University of Toledo, 1987.

51. Cooper, David H. "Identification of Critical Behaviors in Kindergarten." Ph.D. diss., University of North Carolina at Camp Hill, 1984.

52. Coopersmith, S. *The Antecedents of Self-Esteem.* San Francisco: W. H. Freeman, 1967.

53. Covington, Martin V. "The Motive for Self-Worth." In *Research on Motivation*, edited by Russell Ames and Carole Ames, vol. 1, 77-113. Orlando, Fla.: Academic Press, 1984.

54. Cruickshank, D. B. *Models for the Preparation of American's Teachers.* Bloomington, Ind.: Phi Delta Kappa Educational Foundation, 1985.

55. Cunningham, Patricia M. "Teachers' Correction Responses to Black Dialect Miscues which Are Non-Meaning-Changing." *Reading Research* 12, no. 3 (Summer 1977): 637-53.

56. Douglas, J. W. B. *The Home and the School.* London: MacGibbon and Kee, 1964.

57. Douglas, J. W. B.; Ross, J. M.; and Simpson, H. R. *All Our Future.* London: Davies, 1968.

58. Downing, John, and Leong, Che Kan. *Psychology of Reading.* New York: Macmillan, 1982.

59. Doyle, W. "The Knowledge Base for Adaptive Instruction: A Perspective from Classroom Research." In *Adapting Instruction to Individual Differences*, edited by M. C. Wang and H. J. Walberg, 91-102. Berkeley, Calif.: McCutchan, 1985.

60. Druian, Greg, and Butler, Jocelyn. "Effective School Practices and At-Risk Youth: What the Research Shows." School Improvement Research Series, Topical Synthesis #1. Portland, Oreg.: Northwest Regional Educational Laboratory, 1987.

61. Dunn, Rita. "Teaching Students through Their Individual Learning Styles: A Research Report." *Student Learning Styles and Brain Behavior*, 142-51. Reston, Va.: National Association of Secondary School Principals, 1982.

62. Dunst, Carl, J., and Snyder, Scott W. "A Critique of the Utah State University Early Intervention Meta-Analysis Research." *Exceptional Children* 53, no. 3 (November 1986): 269-76.

63. *Education and Economic Progress: Toward a National Education Policy: The Federal Role.* New York: Carnegie Corporation of New York, 1983.

64. Edwards, Janice D. "A Follow-up Study of Early Identified Emotionally Disturbed Children Following Treatment in a Theraputic Nursery School Program." Ph.D. diss., American University, 1985.

65. Elkind, David. *Miseducation: Preschoolers at Risk.* New York: Knopf, 1988.

66. Engman, L. A. "Capitalism Advancing All People Despite Unequal Sharing of Wealth." *Pittsburgh Press*, March 15, 1985, B3.

67. Entwisle, D. R. "Social Class Differences in Learning to Read." Paper presented at a symposium of Interdisciplinary Institute in Child Development, University of Delaware, June 17 to July 12, 1974.

68. *The Failure of Our Public Schools: The Causes and a Solution.* Dallas: National Center for Policy Analysis, 1983.

69. "Falk School Nongraded Personalized Progress Plan." Pittsburgh: University of Pittsburgh, 1968.

70. Felt, Marilyn C. *Improving Our Schools.* Newton, Mass.: Educational Development Center, 1985.

71. Fine, Marvin J., ed. *The Second Handbook on Parent Education.* San Diego: Academic Press, 1988.

72. Finkelhor, David. *Sexually Victimized Children.* New York: Free Press, 1979.

73. Fisher, C. W.; Berliner, D. C.; Filby, N.; Marliave, R.; Cahan, L. S.; and Dishaw, M. M. "Teaching Behaviors, Academic Learning Time, and Student Achievement: An Overview." In *Time to Learn,* edited by C. Denham and A. Lieberman, 7-32. Washington, D.C.: National Institute of Education, 1980.

74. Fordham, Signithia, and Ogbu, John U. "Black Students' School Success: Coping with the 'Burden of Acting White.' " *Urban Review* 18: 183.

75. Foster, Glen G.; Schmidt, Carl R.; and Sabatino, David. "Teacher Expectations and the Label 'Learning Disabled.' " *Journal of Learning Disabilities* 9 (February 1976): 111-14.

76. Fox, B. "Literacy and State Funded Prekindergarten Programs: Speaking Out on the Issues." *Reading Teacher* 41, no. 1 (October 1987): 58-64.

77. Gaa, John W. "The Effects of Individual Goal-Setting Conferences on Academic Achievement and Modification of Locus of Control Orientation." *Psychology in the Schools* 16, no. 4 (October 1979): 591-97.

78. Gabriel, Roy M., and Rasp, Alfred, Jr. "Educating Washington's At-Risk Youth: A Synthesis of Policies and Recent Studies." Portland, Oreg.: Northwest Regional Educational Laboratory, 1986.

79. Gadway, C. *Right to Read: Functional Literacy.* Denver: National Assessment of Educational Progress, 1976.

80. Gallup, A. M., and Clark, D. L. "The 19th Annual Gallup Poll of the Public's Attitudes toward the Public Schools." *Phi Delta Kappan* 68, no. 1 (September 1987): 17-30.

81. Gallup, G. G., and Gallup, A. M. *The Great American Success Story*. Homewood, Ill.: Dow Jones-Irwin, 1986.

82. Gardner, H. *Frames of Mind: The Theory of Multiple Intelligence*. New York: Basic Books (Harper & Row), 1983.

83. Gates, Nancy E. "The Effects of the South Carolina Home-Based Parent Education Programs on Readiness for First Grade Instruction and Home Support." Ph.D. diss., University of South Carolina, 1985.

84. Gavzer, B. "Must Kids Be Bad?" *Parade Magazine*, March 9, 1986, 8.

85. Givens, Robert P. "The Relationship between Preschool Attendance, Reading Achievement, and Pupil Behavior." Ph.D. diss., Pepperdine University, 1984.

86. Goddard, H. E. *The Kallikak Family*. New York: Macmillan, 1912.

87. Gollnick, Donna M, and Chinn, Philip C. *Multicultural Education in a Pluralistic Society*. Columbus, Ohio: Charles E. Merrill, 1986.

88. Golub, Judith S. "Abusive and Nonabusive Parents' Perceptions of Their Children's Behavior: An Attitude Analysis." Ph.D. diss., University of California at Los Angeles, 1984.

89. Good, Thomas L., and Brophy, Jere E. *Looking in Classrooms*. New York: Harper & Row, 1987.

90. Goodlad, John I. "Structure, Process, and an Agenda." In *The Ecology of School Renewal*. Chicago: National Society for the Study of Education, University of Chicago Press, 1987.

91. _____. *A Place Called School: Prospects for the Future*. New York: McGraw-Hill, 1984.

92. Goodson, Floyd L. "Factors Related to Success in Reading by Disadvantaged Children." Ph.D. diss., University of Arizona, 1974.

93. Goodwin, W., and Sanders, J. "An Exploratory Study of the Effect of Selected Variables upon Teacher Expectations of Pupils' Success." Paper presented at meeting of American Educational Research Association, 1969.

94. Gordon, E. W.; DeStefano, L.; and Shipman, S. "Characteristics of Learning Persons and Adaptations of Learning Environments." In *Adapting Instruction to Individual Differences*, edited by M. S. Wang and H. J. Walberg, 44-65. Berkeley, Calif.: McCutchan, 1985.

95. Gough, P. B. "The Key to Improving Schools: An Interview with William Glasser." *Phi Delta Kappan* 68, no. 9 (May 1987): 656-62.

96. Griffin, George W. "Childhood Risk Indicators in Violent Aggressive Adolescents." Ph.D. diss., University of North Carolina at Camp Hill, 1984.

97. Griggs, Shirley A. "Counseling Middle School Students for Their Individual Learning Styles." *Student Learning Styles and Brain Behavior*, 19-24. Reston, Va.: National Association of Secondary School Principals, 1982.

98. Gump, Paul V. "Operating Environments in Schools of Open and Traditional Design." *School Review* 82 (August 1974): 575-93.

99. Hagstrum, Susan A. "Vocational Adjustment of Former Students with General Learning Difficulties." Ph.D. diss., University of Minnesota, 1987.

100. Hahn, Andrew. "Reaching Out to America's Dropouts: What to Do?" *Phi Delta Kappan* 69, no. 4 (December 1987): 256-63.

101. Hanline, Mary F., and Carola, Murray. "Integrating Severely Handicapped Children into Regular Public Schools." *Phi Delta Kappan* 66, no. 4 (December 1984): 273-76.

102. Hannah, Jane N. "The Relationship of a Kindergarten Intervention Program to Reading Readiness, Language Skills, and Reading Achievement." Ph.D. diss., George Peabody College for Teachers of Vanderbilt University, 1985.

103. Harbaugh, Mary. "Who Will Teach the Class of 2000?" *Instructor* 95 (September 1985): 31-36.

104. Hare, R. D. "Twenty Years of Experience with the Checkley Psychopath." In *Unmasking the Psychopath*, edited by W. H. Reid, J. I. Walker, and J. W. Bonner III, 3-27. New York: W. W. Norton, 1986.

105. Harman, David. "Keeping Up in America." *Wilson Quarterly* 10, no. 2 (Spring 1986): 116-31.

106. Harris, Albert J., and Sipay, Edward R. *How to Increase Reading Abiltiy.* New York: Longman, 1985.

107. Harris, Mary M. "Family Forces for Early School Development of Language Fluency and Beginning Reading." In *Mobilizing Family Forces for Worldwide Reading Success*, edited by H. W. Sartain, 55-73. Newark, Del.: International Reading Association, 1981.

108. Haskell, Martin R., and Yablonsky, Lewis. *Juvenile Delinquency.* Boston: Houghton Mifflin, 1982.

109. Hawkins, David, et al. "Childhood Predictors and the Prevention of Adolescent Substance Abuse." *Etiology of Drug Abuse: Implications for Prevention*, NIDA. Washington, D.C.: U.S. Government Printing Office, 1985.

110. Hawley, R. A. "School Children and Drugs: The Fancy That Has Not Passed." Kappan Special Report. *Phi Delta Kappan* 68, no. 9 (May 1987): K1-K8.

111. Heimberger, Mary J. "Continued Focus on Families for Cultural Appreciation, Curriculum Planning, and Tutoring in Reading." In *Mobilizing Family Forces for Worldwide Reading Success*, edited by H. W. Sartain, 74-86. Newark, Del.: International Reading Association, 1981.

112. Henderson, Ronald W. "Environmental Predictors of Academic Performance of Disadvantaged Mexican-American Children." *Journal of Consulting and Clinical Psychology* 38 (April 1972): 297.

113. Hersch, P. "Coming of Age on City Streets." *Psychology Today* 22, no. 1 (January 1988): 28-37.

114. Hey, Robert P. "Cavazos Urges Action to Reduce Minority Dropout Rate." *Christian Science Monitor*, February 1, 1989, 8.

115. ———. "U.S. Army Data Show AIDS Virus Is a Growing Teenage Problem." *Christian Science Monitor*, May 2, 1988.

116. Hill, Gerald D. "An Experimental Investigation into the Interaction between Modality Preference and Instructional Mode in Learning Spelling Words by Upper-Elementary Learning Disabled Students." Ph.D. diss., North Texas State University, 1987.

117. Hillson, Maurie, et al. "A Controlled Experiment Evaluating the Effects of Nongraded Organization on Pupil Achievement." *Journal of Educational Research* 58 (July/August 1964): 548-50.

118. Hirschi, Travis. *Causes of Delinquency*. Berkeley, Calif.: University of California Press, 1969.

119. Hoffman, William R. "Nature and Nurture: Reprise of a Classic Experiment." *University of Minnesota Update* 14, no. 7 (August 1987): 2-3.

120. Hollingsworth, Paul M. "An Experimental Approach to the Impress Method of Teaching Reading." *Reading Teacher* 31 (March 1978): 624-26.

121. Horodezky, Betty. "Family Forces for Preschool Development of Health, Vocabulary, and Perceptual Skills." In *Mobilizing Family Forces for Worldwide Reading Success,* edited by H. W. Sartain, 44-54. Newark, Del.: International Reading Association, 1981.

122. Hughes, Jan N. *Cognitive Behavior Therapy with Children in Schools*. New York: Pergamon Press, 1988.

123. Hurley, Dan. "Arresting Delinquency." *Phi Delta Kappan* 19, no. 3 (March 1985): 64-68.

124. Ingram, Vivien. "Flint Evaluates Its Primary Cycle." *Elementary School Journal* 61 (November 1960): 76-80.

125. Jensen, Arthur R. *Educability and Group Differences*. New York: Harper, 1973.

126. Johnson, Deborah J. "Identity Formation and Racial Coping Strategies of Black Children and Their Parents: A Stress and Coping Paradigm." Ph.D. diss., Northwestern University, 1987.

127. Johnson, D. W., and Johnson, R. T. "Cooperative Learning and Adaptive Education." In *Adapting Instruction to Individual Differences*, edited by M. C. Wang and H. J. Walberg, 105-34. Berkeley, Calif.: McCutchan, 1985.

128. Johnson, Lloyd D., et al. *Monitoring the Future*, NIDA. Washington, D.C.: U.S. Government Printing Office, 1986.

129. Johnson, Steven M. "A Study of Special Needs Learners and Their Employment Success upon Graduation from Carpentry Programs in Selected Vocational High Schools in Western Massachusetts." Ph.D. diss., University of Massachusetts, 1987.

130. Jones, Beau Fly. "Toward Redefining Models of Curriculum and Instruction for Students at Risk." In *At-Risk Students and Thinking: Perspectives from Research*, edited by Barbara Z. Presseisen, 76-103. Washington, D.C.: National Education Association and Research for Better Schools, 1988.

131. Jones, Coryl L., and Battjes, Robert J., eds. *Etiology of Drug Abuse: Implications and Prevention*, NIDA. Washington, D.C.: U.S. Government Printing Office, 1985.

132. Jones, Daisy M. "Experiment in Adaptation to Individual Differences." *Journal of Educational Psychology* 30 (May 1948): 257-72.

133. Kagan, Sharon L. "'Early Care and Education: Tackling the Tough Issues." *Phi Delta Kappan* 70, no. 6 (February 1989): 433-39.

134. Karmin, M. W. "Economic Outlook: Junk-food Jobs and Presidential Tasks." *U.S. News and World Report*, August 15, 1988, 46.

135. Karweit, Nancy. "Time Spent, Time Needed, and Adaptive Instruction." In *Adapting Instruction to Individual Differences*, edited by M. C. Wang and H. J. Walberg, 281-97. Berkeley, Calif.: McCutchan, 1985.

136. Katz, Jack. *Seductions of Crime: Moral and Sensual Attractions in Doing Evil*. New York: Basic Books, 1989.

137. Kay, Linda A. H. "Crisis and Community: A Study of Juvenile Delinquents." Ph.D. diss., University of Mississippi, 1987.

138. Kearns, John R. "The Impact of Systematic Feedback on Students' Self-Esteem." Ph.D. diss., University of Alabama, 1987.

139. Keefe, James W. "Assessing Student Learning Styles: An Overview." *Student Learning Styles and Brain Behavior*, 43-53. Reston, Va.: National Association of Secondary School Principals, 1982.

140. _____. "School Applications of the Learning Style Concept." *Student Learning Styles: Diagnosing and Prescribing Programs*. Reston, Va.: National Association of Secondary School Principals, 1979.

141. Keller, Clayton E., and Hallahan, Daniel P. *Learning Disabilities: Issues and Instructional Interventions*. What Research Says to the Teacher Series. Washington, D.C.: National Education Association, 1987.

142. Kenney, A. M. "Teen Pregnancy: An Issue for Schools." *Phi Delta Kappan* 68, no. 10 (June 1987): 728-36.

143. Ketcham, Clay A. "The Home Background and Reader Self-Concept Which Relate to Reading Achievement." Ph.D. diss., Lehigh University, 1966.

144. Klausmeier, R. J. "A Design for Improving Secondary Education." In *Adapting Instruction to Individual Differences*, edited by M. C. Wang and H. J. Walberg, 160-90. Berkeley, Calif.: McCutchan, 1985.

145. Kleinfield, J. *Effective Teachers of Indian and High School Indian Students*. Fairbanks, Alaska: Institute of Social, Economic, and Government Research, 1974.

146. Klempner, Jack, and Parker, Rodger D. *Juvenile Delinquency and Juvenile Justice*. New York: Franklin Watts, 1981.

147. Kohler, Patricia A. "The Effects of Teacher Expectations and a Student Achievement Model on the Achievement and Self-Concepts of Mildly Handicapped Students Receiving Resource Room Instruction." Ph.D. diss., Memphis State University, 1987.

148. Kohn, A. "David and Roger's Modest Proposal." *University of Minnesota Update* 15, no. 4 (April 1988): 1.

149. _____. *No Contest: The Case Against Competition*. Boston: Houghton Mifflin, 1987.

150. Kunisawa, Byron N. "A Nation in Crisis: The Dropout Dilemma." *NEA Today*, Special Edition (January 1988): 61-65.

151. Kurtines, William M., and Gewirtz, Jacob L. *Moral Development through Social Interaction*. New York: John Wiley and Sons, 1987.

152. Lamphear, Vivian S. "Social Problem-Solving Skills and Psychosocial Adjustment of Children-at-Risk for Physical Abuse." Ph.D. diss., State University of New York at Stony Brook, 1987.

153. Lehr, Judy B., and Harris, Hazel W. *At-Risk, Low-Achieving Students in the Classroom*. Analysis and Action Series. Washington, D.C.: National Education Association, 1988.

154. Lewis, A. C. "Barriers in the Path of the Non-college-bound." *Phi Delta Kappan* 69, no. 6 (February 1988): 396-7.

155. Lipsitz, Joan. *Successful Schools for Young Adolescents*. New Brunswick, N.J.: Transaction Books, 1984.

156. London, P. "Character Education and Clinical Intervention: A Paradigm for U.S. Schools." *Phi Delta Kappan* 68, no. 9 (May 1987): 667-73.

157. Ludlow, Barbara L. "Teaching the Learning Disabled." PDK Fastback No. 169. Bloomington, Ind.: Phi Delta Kappa, 1982.

158. MacGillis, D., with ABC News. *Crime in America: The ABC Report*. Radnor, Pa.: Chilton Book Co., 1983.

159. Maeroff, Gene I. "Withered Hopes, Stillborn Dreams: The Dismal Panorama of Urban Schools." *Phi Delta Kappan* 69, no. 9 (May 1988): 632-38.

160. Maez, Angelita. "The Effects of Two-Parent Training Programs on Parental Attitudes and Self-Concepts of Mexican American Mothers." Ph.D. diss., University of Southern California, 1987.

161. Magid, Ken, and McKelvey, Carole A. *High Risk: Children without a Conscience*. New York: Bantam, 1987.

162. Mandel, Harvey P., and Marcus, Sander I. *The Psychology of Underachievement: Differential Diagnosis and Differential Treatment*. New York: John Wiley and Sons, 1988.

163. Marquand, R. "Dealing with Problems of 'At Risk' Youth." *Christian*

Science Monitor, November 18, 1985, 35ff.

164. Martin, L., and Pavan, B. "Current Research on Open Space, Nongrading, Vertical Grouping, and Team Teaching." *Phi Delta Kappan* 57 (1976): 310-15.

165. Mastropieri, Margo A.; Scruggs, Thomas E.; and Levin, Joel R. "Maximizing What Exceptional Students Can Learn: A Review of Research on the Keyword Method and Related Mnemonic Techniques." *Remedial and Special Education* 6, no. 2 (March/April 1985): 39-45.

166. Mathews, Jay. *Escalante: The Best Teacher in America.* New York: Henry Holt, 1988.

167. McDonald-Jacobs, Rose-Alma J. "A Study of School Attitude of Akwesasne Mohawk Students Who Attend Primary Schools in Canada and the United States." Ph.D. diss., Pennsylvania State University, 1987.

168. McHenry, Patrick C., et al. "The Role of Drugs in Adolescent Suicide Attempts." *Suicide and Life-Threatening Behavior* 13, no. 3 (Fall 1983): 131-35.

169. McMichael, P. "Reading Difficulties, Behavior and Social Status." *Journal of Educational Psychology* 72 (1980): 76-86.

170. Mednick. S. "Crime in the Family Tree." *Psychology Today* 19, no. 3 (March 1985): 58-68.

171. "More Unmarried Couples Living Together." *Pittsburgh Press*, May 13, 1988.

172. Morgan, M., and Gross, L. "Television and Academic Achievement." *Journal of Broadcasting* 24 (1980): 117-32.

173. *A Nation at Risk: The Imperative for Educational Reform.* Washington, D.C.: National Commission on Excellence in Education, U.S. Department of Education, 1983.

174. Needham, Nancy R. "Kids Who Kill and Are Killed." *NEA Today* 6, no. 7 (February 1988): 10-11.

175. Neuman, Susan B. "The Displacement Effect: Assessing the Relation between Television Viewing and Reading Performance." *Reading Research Quarterly* 23, no. 4 (1988): 414-40.

176. "Nongraded School Organization." *National Education Association Research Bulletin* 43 (October 1965): 93-95.

177. Oakes, Jeannie. "Tracking: Can Schools Take a Different Route?" *NEA Today* Special Edition (January 1988): 41-47.

178. Ohio Department of Education Task Force. *Ohio's Classroom of the Future: A Progress Report.* Columbus, Ohio: Ohio Department of Education, 1988.

179. Otto, Wayne; Wolf, Anne; and Eldridge, Roger G. "Managing Instruction." In *Handbook of Reading Research*, edited by P. David Pearson, 799-828. New York: Longman, 1984.

180. Paladry, J. M. "What Teachers Believe, What Children Achieve." *Elementary School Journal* 69 (1969): 370-74.

181. Patros, Philip G., and Shamoo, Tonia K. *Depression and Suicide in Children and Adolescents: Prevention, Intervention, and Postvention.* Boston: Allyn and Bacon, 1989.

182. Pener, Darlene E. "An Exploratory Study of the Behaviors and Attitudes of Regular Class Teachers toward Special Needs Pupils Integrated in Their Classes." Ph.D. diss., Univeristy of British Columbia, 1986.

183. Perpich, Rudy. "In Education, One-on-One Works." *Christian Science Monitor*, January 30, 1989, 19.

184. Pfeifer, Jerilyn K. "Teenage Suicide: What Can the Schools Do?" PDK Fastback No. 234. Bloomington, Ind.: Phi Delta Kappa, 1986.

185. Pies, Diane L. "The Relationship between Children's and Teachers' Perceptions of Students' Learning Styles in a Black, Low SES Elementary School Population." Ph.D. diss., University of Pennsylvania, 1987.

186. Presseisen, Barbara Z., ed. *At-Risk Students and Thinking: Perspectives from Research.* Washington, D.C.: National Education Association and Research for Better Schools, 1988.

187. Price, Gary E. "Learning Style Inventory Development and Continuing Research." *Student Learning Styles and Brain Behavior.* Reston, Va.: National Association of Secondary School Principals, 1982.

188. Rabow, G. "The Cooperative Edge." *Psychology Today* 22, no. 1 (January 1988): 54-58.

189. Raffini, James P. *Student Apathy: The Protection of Self-Worth.* What Research Says to the Teacher Series. Washington, D.C.: National Education Association, 1988.

190. Ralph, John. "Improving Education for the Disadvantaged: Do We Know Whom to Help?" *Phi Delta Kappan* 70, no. 5 (January 1989): 395-401.

191. Reed, Keflyn X. "Expectation vs. Ability: Junior College Reading Skills." *Journal of Reading* 32, no. 6 (March 1989): 537-41.

192. Reitz, James D. "The Effect of Goal-Setting Activities on Locus of Control and Achievement of Learning Disabled Middle School Students." Ph.D. diss., University of Alabama, 1984.

193. Reynolds, W. M. "Depression in Children and Adolescents: Phenomenology, Evaluation and Treatment." *School Psychology Review* 13 (1984): 171-82.

194. Rist, Ray C. "Students' Social Class and Teacher Expectations: The Self-Fulfilling Prophecy in Ghetto Education." *Harvard Educational Review* 40 (August 1970): 411-51.

195. Rosenshine, B. V. "How Time Is Spent in Elementary Classrooms." In *Time to Learn*, edited by C. Denham and A. Lieberman, 107-26. Washington, D.C.: National Institute of Education, 1980.

196. Rosenshine, B. V., and Stevens, R. "Classroom Instruction in Reading." In *Handbook of Reading Research*, edited by P. David Pearson, 745-98. New York: Longman, 1984.

197. Rosenthal, R., and Jacobson, L. *Pygmalion in the Classroom: Teacher Expectation and Pupils' Intellectual Development*. New York: Holt, Rinehart, and Winston, 1968.

198. Rosenthal, P. A., and Rosenthal, S. "Suicidal Behavior by Preschool Children." *American Journal of Psychiatry* 141, no. 4 (1984): 520-25.

199. Rupley, William H., and Blair, Timothy R. "Research Revisited: Teacher Effectiveness Research in Reading Instruction: Early Efforts to Present Focus." *Reading Psychology* 2 (Fall 1980): 49-56.

200. Rutter, M., Tizard, J., and Whitmore, K., eds. *Education, Health, and Behavior*. London: Longman, 1970.

201. Sartain, Harry W. "Research Summary: Family Contributions to Reading Achievement." In *Mobilizing Family Forces for Worldwide Reading Success*, edited by H. W. Sartain, 4-18. Newark, Del.: International Reading Association, 1981.

202. _____. "Instruction of Disabled Learners: A Reading Perspective." *Journal of Learning Disabilities* 9, no. 8 (October 1976): 489-97.

203. _____. "Organizational Patterns of Schools and Classrooms for Reading Instruction." In *Innovation and Change in Reading Instruction*, edited by Helen M. Robinson, 195-236. Chicago: National Society for the Study of Education, University of Chicago Press, 1968.

204. Sartain, Harry W., and Seamen, Conrad. "Falk School Checklist of Impediments to Communication and Learning." Pittsburgh: University of Pittsburgh, n.d.

205. Saxe, Joseph E. "Using Preschool Screening Data to Predict Educational Outcomes." Ph.D. diss., Pennsylvania State University, 1987.

206. Schafer, W. E., and Polk, Kenneth. "Delinquency and the Schools." *Task Force Report: Juvenile Delinquency and Youth Crime*. Washington, D.C.: U.S. Government Printing Office, 1967.

207. Sciara, Frank J., and Jantz, Richard K. "Father Absence and Its Apparent Effect on the Reading Achievement of Black Children from Low Income Families." *Journal of Negro Education* 43 (Spring 1974): 221-27.

208. Searls, D. T.; Mead, N. A.; and Ward, B. "The Relationship of Students' Reading Skills to TV Watching, Leisure Time Reading, and Homework." *Journal of Reading* 29, no. 2 (November 1985): 158-62.

209. Seitz, Victoria. *Social Class and Ethnic Group Differences in Learning to Read*. Series on the Development of the Reading Process. Newark, Del.: International Reading Association, 1977.

210. Serwer, Blanche L. "The Relation between Parent-Child Interaction and Inadequacy in College Reading and Study." Paper presented at Congress

of Inter-American Society of Psychology, Mexico City, December 1967. ED 016 589.

211. Shaw, Clifford R., and McKay, Henry D. "Social Factors in Juvenile Delinquency." In *Report on Causes of Crime*. National Commission on Law Observance and Enforcement. Washington, D.C.: U.S. Government Printing Office, 1931.

212. Short, James F., Jr.; Rivera, Ramon; and Tennyson, Ray A. "Perceived Opportunities, Gang Membership, and Delinquency." *American Sociological Review* 30 (February 1965): 56-67.

213. Shuy, Roger W., and Frederick, William. "Stereotyped Attitudes of Selected English Dialect Communities." In *Language Attitudes: Current Trends and Prospects,* edited by R. W. Shuy and R. W. Fasolds, 85-96. Washington, D.C.: Georgetown University Press, 1973.

214. Silvernail, David L. *Developing Positive Student Self-Concept.* Analysis and Action Series. Washington, D.C.: National Education Association, 1985.

215. Skapski, Mary K. "Upgraded Primary Reading Program: An Objective Evaluation." *Elementary School Journal* 61 (1960): 41–45.

216. Slavin, R. E. "Team-Assisted Individualization: A Cooperative Learning Solution for Adaptive Instruction in Mathematics." In *Adapting Instruction to Individual Differences*, edited by M. C. Wang and H. J. Walberg, 236-53. Berkeley, Calif.: McCutchan, 1985.

217. Smith, Carl B. "The Expanding Role of Parents." *Reading Teacher* 42, no. 1 (October 1988): 68-69.

218. Smith. R. A. "A Teacher's Views on Cooperative Learning." *Phi Delta Kappan* 68, no. 9 (May 1987): 663-66.

219. Smolowe, J. "The Drug Thugs." *Time* 131 (17 March 1988): 28-37.

220. Snee, Beth Musser. "The Effects of Parent-Guided Language Activities on Reading Achievement of Children after First Grade." Ph.D. diss., University of Pittsburgh, 1981.

221. Sowell, Thomas. *Ethnic America.* New York: Basic Books, 1981.

222. Sprinthall, Richard C., and Sprinthall, Norman. *Educational Psychology: A Developmental Approach.* Reading, Mass.: Addison-Wesley, 1981.

223. Stackhouse, Thomas W. "A Communication Analysis of the Art of Being Stupid: A Family Systems and Communication Approach to the Study of Families with Children Having Reading Problems." Ph.D. diss., University of Georgia, 1974.

224. Stedman, L. C., and Kaestle, C. F. "Literacy and Reading Performance in the United States, from 1880 to the Present." *Reading Research Quarterly* 22, no. 1 (Winter 1987): 8-46.

225. Steele, B. "WPIC Developing Therapies to Treat Antisocial Children." *University Times* 20, no. 5 (October 1987): 6.

226. Stein, Paul S. "Family Life, Social Class, and High School Achievement: A Study of Successful Boys from White Working-Class Families." Ph.D. diss., Boston University, 1988.

227. Stewart, D. M. *Education Week*, June 17, 1987, 18.

228. Stillwell, W. E., and Barclay, J. R. "The Effects of Affective Education Interventions in the Elementary School." *Psychology in the Schools* 16 (1979): 80-87.

229. Strain, Phillip S., and Smith, Barbara J. "A Counter-Interpretation of Early Intervention Effects: A Response to Casto and Mastropieri." *Exceptional Children* 53, no. 3 (November 1986): 260-65.

230. Strother, D. B. "Preschool Children in Public Schools: Good Investment? Or Bad?" *Phi Delta Kappan* 69, no. 4 (December 1987): 304-8.

231. Surgeon General's Scientific Advisory Committee on TV and Social Behavior. *TV and Adolescent Aggressiveness*, Vol. 3. Washington, D.C.: U.S. Government Printing Office, 1972.

232. Swartz, F. "Supporting or Subverting Learning: Peer Group Patterns in Four Tracked Schools." *Anthropology and Education Quarterly* 12 (1981): 99-121.

233. Swoyer, Mary E. "A Study of the Effects of a Language Development Program with Parent Involvement on Language Achievement of Low-Level Preschool Children." Ph.D. diss., Temple University, 1985.

234. Taglianetti, Thomas J. "Reading Failure: A Predictor of Delinquency." *Juvenile Justice* 12 (February 1975): 46.

235. Teens' Lifestyle Too Hard and Fast, Study Says." *Pittsburgh Press,* August 9, 1988, A3.

236. Thrasher, Frederic M. *The Gang.* Chicago: University of Chicago Press, 1926.

237. Topping, K. "Paired Reading: A Powerful Technique for Parent Use." *Reading Teacher* 40, no. 7 (March 1987): 608–14.

238. Tower, Cynthia C. *Child Abuse and Neglect.* Washington, D.C.: National Education Association, 1987.

239. Towers, Richard L. *How Schools Can Help Combat Student Drug and Alcohol Abuse.* Washington, D.C.: National Education Association, 1987.

240. Trotter, Robert J. "Robert J. Sternberg: Three Heads Are Better than One." *Psychology Today* 19, no. 8 (August 1986): 56-62.

241. Uttero, D. A. "Activating Comprehension through Cooperative Learning." *Reading Teacher* 41 no. 4 (January 1988): 390-95.

242. "Violent Behavior All in the Mind?" *Pittsburgh Press*, May 28, 1986.

243. Walberg, Herbert. "Families as Partners in Educational Productivity." *Phi Delta Kappan* 65, no. 6 (February 1984): 397-400.

244. Wang, M. C., and Walberg, H. J., eds. *Adapting Instruction to Individual Differences.* Berkeley, Calif.: McCutchan, 1985.

245. Watkins, Betty D. "Parent Education Needs as Expressed by Parents of Young Handicapped Children." Ph. D. diss., Texas Woman's University, 1984.

246. Watson, J. B., and Rayner, R. "Conditioned Emotional Reactions." *Journal of Experimental Psychology* 3, no. 8 (1921).

247. Wayson, William W., with Pinnell, G. S.; and Landis, D. *Up from Excellence: The Impact of the Excellence Movement on Schools.* Bloomington, Ind.: Phi Delta Kappa Educational Foundation, 1988.

248. Weiner, B., and Kukla, A. "An Attributional Analysis of Achievement Motivation." *Journal of Personality and Social Psychology* 15 (1970): 1-20.

249. Weir, Beth. "A Research Base for Prekindergarten Literacy Programs." *Reading Teacher* 42, no. 7 (March 1989): 456-60.

250. Wesley, Wayman L. "A Study of the Effects of Father-Presence or Father-Absence on the Self-Concept, Locus of Control, Family Relations, and School Relations of Emotionally Disturbed Adolescent Boys." Ph. D. diss., East Texas State University, 1984.

251. "What Works in Reading?" *EPIEgram.* Stoney Brook, N.Y.: EPIE Institute, 1979.

252. *Why Do Some Schools Succeed?* The Phi Delta Kappa study of exceptional elementary schools. Bloomington, Ind.: Phi Delta Kappa, 1980.

253. Wickman, Peter, and Whitten, Phillip. *Criminology: Perspectives on Crime and Criminality.* Lexington, Mass.: D. C. Heath, 1980.

254. Wielkiewicz, Richard M. *Behavior Management in the Schools: Principles and Procedures.* New York: Pergamon Press, 1986.

255. Wigfield, Allan, and Asher, Steven R. "Social and Environmental Influences on Reading." In *Handbook of Reading Research,* edited by P. David Pearson, 423-52. New York: Longman, 1984.

256. Wilkinson, Karen. "The Broken Family and Juvenile Delinquency: Scientific Explanation of Idiology." *Social Problems* 21, no. 5 (June 1974): 726-37.

257. William T. Grant Foundation Commission on Work, Family and Citizenship. "The Forgotten Half: Pathways to Success for America's Youth and Young Families." *Phi Delta Kappan* 70, no. 4 (December 1988): 281-89.

258. Wilson, William J. *The Truly Disadvantaged.* Chicago: University of Chicago Press, 1988.

259. Wiseman, S. "Educational Deprivation and Disadvantage." In *Educational Research in Britain,* edited by H. J. Butcher, vol. 1. London: University of London Press, 1968.

260. Wolfgang, M. E.; Figlio, R. M.; and Sellin, T. *Delinquency in a Birth Cohort.* Chicago: University of Chicago Press, 1972.

261. Wood, K. D. "Fostering Cooperative Learning in Middle and Secondary Classrooms." *Journal of Reading* 31, no. 1 (October 1987): 10-16.

262. Woodring, Paul. "A New Approach to the Dropout Problem." *Phi Delta Kappan* 70, no. 6 (February 1989): 468-69.

263. Yale Bush Center Infant Care Leave Project. *Facts on Parents in the Workforce and Infant Care.* New Haven, Conn.: Yale Bush Center, 1985.

264. "Youth Indicators 1988: Trends in the Well-being of American Youth." Washington, D.C.: U. S. Government Printing Office, 1988.